Great American
Food Shortage

J.R. Fisher

Printed in the United States of America First

Printing, 2017

II

Table of Contents

IV

Dedication:

Dedicated to my wife Jessica who has supported me through all of my business ventures. Her support and love has always been there and I want to take this opportunity to thank her. I love you very much Jessica.

Introduction:

I want to start off by telling you I am not a fortuneteller or someone who has some "inside" knowledge of the inner workings of the world.

I don't share this information to scare you or to stir up negative sentiment towards any country or government. I share this information and have written this book because I want to wake up as many people as possible so that they can prepare for the future. A future that is very uncertain, which if you are not prepared for it, can take you by surprise and may take your life.

If I can accomplish helping, by educating more people, then I feel I can contribute to the preparedness of millions of people, and hopefully save lives, and prevent some of the hysteria that is certain to occur when the food shortages occur.

How did I come to figure out what was happening? I guess I do have a little insight since I am in the food industry. I am constantly hit by price increases on various ingredients, and I tend to dig deeper to find out why these occur. The answers I have found over the years are nothing short of frightening. If you are reading this book, I need to congratulate you because you are a very small segment of the population that has chosen to take it upon themselves to be proactive.

You are probably reading this book because you know it's time to worry. In fact, there never has been a more turbulent time as now. Who knows what brought you to this point in your life? Maybe you have just matured or, for some reason, you have become more aware of your surroundings and world events.

Yes, being more aware can be scary because you finally realize there are problems in the world ... big problems. Many, if not   most of these problems, you can't do anything about. You can't control terrorism, economic collapse, or wars.

The truth is you are right correct to worry. Those feelings of fear and uncertainly are real. You have no control over natural disasters because no one can control the weather, earthquakes, or any natural disaster.

Terrorism has now become a worldwide problem. No country will ever be safe from people who have an agenda to destroy other people lives and sense of security.

I understand you may feel scared, out of control, and unprotected at this point; but, by the time you finish this book, you will, at least, be able to do something about your "own" personal safety.

As you read this book, I will educate you on why you should be concerned, what causes will contribute to the great American food shortage and most importantly what you can personally do   to help protect yourself and your family.

Is it possible that America could prevent the impending food shortages? This is a difficult question to answer, and certainly things could be done to alleviate or stop the food shortage. But, I have more faith in my ability to prepare than I do in the governments that cause these shortages to cure the underlying problems.

By the time you finish this book, you will more empowered, educated and of course, you may experience a great sense of relief because you will be prepared to survive the up-coming   food shortages.

So let's begin our journey into the "The Great American Food Shortage." This will be something, that I am afraid will go down in history as an obvious problem, that most Americans never saw coming, although there are warning signs everywhere.

CHAPTER 1:

Emergencies—
Not Just a Preppers Problem

Prepping - not a FAD

I ant to start off by addressing the face that prepping is NOT A FAD. I hear this over and over and am stunned when I hear people say, "This prepping thing will go away." "It's just popular now because of TV shows, and pretty soon it will burn out." Really? It's not real? Lets go back a few years. Lets pick 50 years ago when we would visit our older relatives. For those of you that are younger, just stick with me for a few minutes as we travel down memory lane.

As a kid, I would visit my relative's homes, and one, in particular, lived in Pennsylvania. They lived in a community in the mountains, and they had a basement stocked with food.

I was intrigued by this room under their house and would explore this dark, dry area and investigate all of the cool things I found there. It had the normal things like lawn equipment and old boxes packed for storage, but it also had many shelves stocked with foods. It had canned vegetables (when I say canned, I refer to the old glass mason jars), fruits and staples like flour, sugar, and salt. They had emergency supplies like flashlights, first aid items, and warm clothing. Now this list is only a few items because the actual list is way too long to put in this section.

One day, I asked them why they had this huge supply of food and supplies, and they responded, "You have to be prepared for emergencies; because if there is a storm or disaster, you have to have what you need. You can't always run down to the store to get what you need." These folks never mentioned that the government would help them because they knew that was not an option they would rely on.

You have to understand this was in the 1960's, and anyone over 40 went through the great depression. They experienced the loss of jobs, money, and food. They KNEW things could go bad fast because they saw it first hand.

In today's world, many of us have not seen a true disaster or economic collapse. We have enjoyed a period of time when most people have always had food in their stomachs and clothes on their backs. They haven't had to do without, so they can't imagine it to be a real thing.

The truth is that "not preparing" is the real fad. If you go back even further in time, like say 60, 70 or even 100 years ago, everyone was prepared. They all stored food from the summer to last through the winter. They depended on their own crops or their neighbors' because the stores, as we know them today, just didn't exist. There weren't convenience stores or grocery stores stocked with every imaginable food.

No, these people were self-sufficient because they HAD to be. These people didn't have the availability of foods and supplies, so they did what they had to do. They PREPARED!

Sure, I am certain some of you who are reading this book have experienced a storm, riot, or even have relocated to America from a region of the world where they didn't have all of these conveniences. And, I would be willing to bet that those are the types of people who do prepare and have a backup plan for when things go bad.

If you have been through some turmoil in your life, then you might realize that things can and do go bad, and you need to prepare for when that happens.

No, preparing is not a FAD; but, what is a FAD is "not preparing." This is a dangerous fad that has caught people off guard when they experienced a situation where food and supplies were not available.

How will emergencies affect you?

Throughout your life, you have probably heard a lot of things about being prepared for an emergency. When you attended school, you learned how to prepare in case of a tornado, fire, or some other disaster. Depending on the region of the country you live in, your local government may hand out pamphlets filled with information meant to educate you in the event of an emergency.

When you see this information, what do you do with it? Do you assume that everything is going to be fine? Do you assume that you will have plenty of time to get everything together, and keep your family safe and sound during the emergency?

Most people will have some of these thoughts in their head. They don't believe emergencies will affect them, and they feel that the effort is not worth their time. They might figure preppers are the only ones who might consider getting things ready, because they feel it will never happen or won't be as bad as they fear. People just don't want to believe disasters will happen to them.

Being prepared for an emergency is not something that just preppers should be worried about. In fact, it should be a problem everyone should be prepared for. Ask yourself, what you would do if a big hurricane, tornado, or other disaster makes getting food difficult in your area? What if there were a food issue in another part of the world, making it difficult for you to get some of the staples that your family depends upon to survive?

At this point, you may think this is never going to happen. You may feel it doesn't matter if a disaster occurs in another part of the world or even in another part of your country. You may also feel there is plenty of food all over the place, and you can get by without the food from another location. What you fail to realize is, in our modern world is that our food supplies are dangerously connected. It is very rare that you would be able to last for long on the foods that are grown in your geographic area. This modern world is so interconnected that when one place has something go wrong, it can begin to affect all the other parts of the world; yes, even your own.

You never know when something could go wrong in another country that could affect your food supply. A corrupt government can take over a country and halt their food production for America. A disease could occur and wipe out a crop for years. Natural disasters are occurring all of the time, and may halt production of food and cause a serious food shortage at any moment.

These situations have occurred throughout the course of history, making it very likely that we will encounter supply chain challenges. Luckily, at this point, there is often more than one option for a food source. We can often make due without certain types of fruits or other small food group. But, issues can arise when some of our staples, or a large majority of our foods, are no longer available. What will you do then? Not a good feeling!

Let's take a look at what would happen to society, or, at least, the society nearest to you if the food supplies started to dwindle without any chance of being replaced. We will take it to the extreme and assume that all food and other items have been taken away and that the stores will no longer be receiving shipments due to some unknown cause.

Everything Shuts Down

The first thing that will happen, when the food supplies run low, is that all the stores are going to be shutting down. Since there won't be any food to deliver, the truckers in the area will be out of a job, and once all the food is off the shelves, the stores will have no reason to stay open. There would not be enough local food to be able to keep up with the demand at local stores around you, so everyone would have to make do with what they have on hand.

Think about how strange this is going to feel. Just walking up and down the streets will look like a ghost town. While some stores may be able to stay open for a short time, most will go out of business once the hoards of people are all done scrambling to buy everything on the shelves.

This is not just going to affect one or two stores in your neighborhood. It will impact every one. Just think about the lack of a food supply. This will close down every store that has any kind of food including convenience stores, grocery stores, and all restaurants. What if the problem goes further and affects other supplies including clothing stores, gas stations? Soon everything else will eventually go out of business as well.

Let this all sink it for a bit. What are you going to do when all of these stores begin to close their doors? And, this isn't going to take as long as you may think. Where are you going to find your clothes or get food for your kids and family members? If you are like most Americans, you don't have a backup plan for when everything does fail. You may have believed that the stores would always carry the items that you needed to stay safe and sound. Now that the stores have failed and are closing, you might not be sure where to turn.

The realization of the mess you are now in is going to start sinking in. You realize you are in deep trouble and will probably do anything to get a food supply and keep yourself and your family safe. Of course, by this point, you will be too late and what comes next will be even more frightening.

Mass Panic

As soon as the news breaks that all food supplies are gone from the area, people are going to start realizing how ill equipped they are to deal with the emergency. Their first thought will be to run out and get as many supplies as they can get their hands on before anyone else. There will be a mass panic everywhere you turn. If you think rationally, you might choose not to go out in all of this craziness; but then you would be completely without food if you hadn't prepared.

Shortly after this news breaks, the stores are going to become a warzone. Everyone will be heading to their local store to snatch up as many products as they can. They will start with the food first; you won't survive long without a lot of food storage on hand to keep you full and satisfied. Some might choose to go after some survival gear or even clothes to stay warm. But, only the lucky few who are able to get there quickly and who can grab their stuff and go, will be able to stay safe in all of this chaos.

In the beginning of the crisis, the stores are only going to have a limited amount of supplies they can offer to the masses. Think of this kind of like Black Friday on steroids. There are thousands of people trying to shop for just a few items. Except, instead of worrying about great deals like with Black Friday, people are worrying about getting supplies to keep them alive. Fights will break out, people will get hurt, and most will leave empty handed and without any idea of what they should do next.

This panic is going to extend to all parts of the city. It will not just be contained in the stores. If you happened to be prepared and have a nice garden in your backyard, someone is probably going to take it from you. While this might seem unimaginable, keep in mind the other person is just doing it to prevent his or her own starvation and to stay alive. There are going to be break-ins into homes and stores all over town in the hopes of getting something to survive.

There are going to be a lot of people who go hungry. Even if the supplies were evenly distributed between everyone in the town, there wouldn't be near enough to last for very long. And, things can get ugly quickly when people start to panic.

Food, Clothing, and Shelter Shortages

Depending on the area you live in, and how much supplies are there, it probably won't take long before your area experiences shortages of shelter, clothing, and food. You won't be able to find anything that you need in the stores to stay safe. At best, there maybe a local farmer who will send in some food for a short period, but this will just create more mass panic at the stores as people try to get ahold of a little bit of food. At worse, there are no more supplies being delivered, and you and your family must find a   new alternative to stay safe.

These shortages are going to last for quite some time. No one knows when the world is going to get back to normal, or when you will be able to go to the store to get the items that you need. This is probably the scariest part. If you knew it was just going to last for a few weeks, you could stay calm and just ration out the supplies you had. But the uncertainty is what really scares people and makes them transition into a full panic.

For those who aren't prepared, this period of time is going to be a nightmare. If you are lucky, you will have a nice full cupboard at home with all the food that you need for a bit. If you are unlucky, you will need to try to go through the craziness at the store in the hopes of finding something to live off of. Things are going to change quickly in your world and those who are able to adapt quickly, or who are prepared ahead of time, are the ones who will live. I know since you're reading this book right now, you are in the small percentage of people who have a plan and may stay safe and alive.

Are You Prepared?

So the question now is, are you prepared? Are you going to be able to make it through the disaster that we just discussed? For most people, the answer will be no. They assume nothing is ever going to happen to them, and they can run off to the store at anytime they wish and get whatever they desire. While this would be an awesome reality to live in, it is not the reality that is going to keep you very safe, nor will it help out with your survival.

But, that is why you are reading this book right now. You know that the threat is real and someday, maybe someday soon, your world is going to be turned upside down by people who may not like Americans, by natural or man made disasters and you need to prepare. And, that is why, in the rest of this book, I'm going to discuss some of the ways you can be prepared in the event one of these disaster occurs. Don't worry, you don't need to be a prepper or a survivalist to pull it off, just be able to prepare before the disaster strikes.

CHAPTER 2:

World Events Are Now America's Problem

At one point, countries used to be little islands all to themselves. They would eat the foods they were able to grow in their own backyards, manufacture their own clothes, and build their own homes. There was very little need for trade or reliance on others; it was common for people to live out on a farm or far away from people and not be reliant on others. On occasion, they may barter a bit with others to get something new. But, most people were self- sufficient and would not need anything that could not be made in their local region.

And, then trade began. It used to be small. The merchants from China were some of the first, bringing silks, spices, and other novelties to the people of Europe. These were expensive because of the long route that they had to take to get from China to any of the European countries. Due to the expense, you had to belong to the richest part of society to participate. This was the beginning of some of the very first international trading that occurred in the world.

Of course, it was also brought about due to the Age of Discovery that began in Europe. European countries wanted to be the biggest and bravest of them all and began to sail the globe to help find new lands and to enable more trade. This is how America was founded; merchants were hoping to find a quicker and easier way to get to China, rather than going on the dangerous journey by foot, or having to go around Africa to get there.

America has spent a lot of its history relying on others for some sort of trade. When America was still the original 13 colonies, it relied on trading with Great Britain. They were not able to get started on their farming and other trade right away because the land was rough and difficult to grow anything. The more fertile land of the Midwest had not yet been discovered. Settlers had to trade for clothing, seeds, and other items just to get them started.

Once America got their Independence, there was a time when they were considered isolationists. There was a reluctance, that many Americans had for generations, to not get involved in the affairs of Europe. This also included restricting of trading with Europe as stiff tariffs were placed on any goods coming into the country. This of course made it more appealing and less expensive to hire American workers. These isolationist days started during the colonial times as the people wanted to be left alone to live their lives and practice their religions.

This isolationism did work out well for the American people in the beginning. It helped them to have a steady growth of jobs since it was cheaper to hire someone here, to make the goods, rather than get them shipped from overseas. It allowed the American people to be self-sufficient and survive off of the land. While it is nice to have more variety from other countries with open relations, America was plenty big enough to have the resources to get out of world trading game.

But, in modern times, the American government has decided it's better to open up the borders. This means that we are getting a lot of our supplies and food from different countries. What will we do when one of these suppliers ends up failing us? Yes of course, we still have a lot of the natural resources, which we had during the isolationism period, but we are not currently set up to, take on all of this production. And, it would take a while before things could get set up and running efficiently. The question is, what would we do until that happens?

This chapter is going to spend some time looking at what occurs when the world becomes globally connected and why this might be detrimental for our future if our trade resources end up failing us.

World Trading Connects Us All

In our modern world, all of the countries are connected into a global economy. Each country is going to help out, in one way or another, to ensure that the others are doing well. Let's look at this kind of like a family. There is a mom, dad, a brother and a sister. One parent is in charge of keeping the house clean, paying bills, and making meals. One parent is in charge of working at a job to help support the family. The kids have to get their homework done so they can go to college and get a good job to help out their parents later on in life. All have to work together to get the chores done in the home.

Now, what happens when one of the people fails? Let's say that the wage earner breaks their leg and are not able to go to work for a long time. Now, the other parent doesn't have the money to pay the bills on time, and they may end up losing their home. Sure, the other parent could go out and get a job, and they probably would but there are medical bills and waiting for a check to come in is going to leave things pretty lean for the whole family. This can be true regardless of which family member who steps out of their duties. All of them must work together to keep things running smoothly, and when one fails, all of them fail. At least, until another arrangement can be made.

In this global economy, all of the countries are going to integrate some of the economies of other countries into their own system so that they are able to work for the common good of everyone. This makes all of them more dependent on each other in order to sustain themselves.

When this type of economy first began, everyone thought that it would be a great idea. Each country could specialize in what it does best while benefiting from the fruits of labor from some of the other countries. A global economy is not completely a bad idea, as long as we understand the entire picture.

For example, what happens when one or two of the countries have a bad year with their crops? Now, all of the countries in the economy are dealing with the loss, even though they held up their end of the bargain and performed in their specialization as agreed. What happens when one country loses a lot of money, and their economy goes down? All of the countries are going to see the same downward trend as well. While this program can bring everyone up together, it is also possible that everyone can go down together.

You remember that time when your favorite fruit wasn't available at the store, even though it was in season? This is most likely because the country you depend on for that fruit was not able to produce as much as they should have. The fruit really isn't that big of a deal since you can just go and pick another one, but if these food shortages began occurring on a large scale, you may find that you are going without many foods you now enjoy.

This type of global economy started during the 1800s. It was during this time that humans began using minerals instead of plants in order to get an energy source and some raw materials. Before this time, animals and plants were the source for fibers, fuel, and food for people. These older methods made it hard to produce more than what you needed because there was only so much energy to go around and plants and animals could only work so much.

But, once people figured out that you could use minerals to power engines and use them to create more food, the global market opened up. Farmers were able to produce much more food in the same amount of time with no extra effort. Now they had more food than they had enjoyed in the past and it was time to sell the extra food to make a profit. Since other farmers in America had the same excess products available, it was time to look for a new market for all of this food. This is how the global economy started to mash together between various countries.

There were some issues with this kind of economy, as I just discussed. First, those countries that were not able to rise to this level of technology were going to be behind. They weren't able to produce more food and other products, and so they weren't able to sell and prosper. In fact, they ended up having to purchase products from the more advanced countries, putting the poorer ones at a bigger disadvantage than they started.

Despite this, the less powerful countries, at least economically, were still able to help. The minerals that were needed to power up machines and make a lot of products often came from the smaller countries with the resorces. They were able to sell these resources to the bigger countries, and that kept the process going. Of course, the smaller countries would then need to purchase the products being made.

This kind of economy expanded during the 20th century. If you have ever shopped online, you know where the economy has gone. Thanks to the Internet, trade barriers went away, and people could purchase more products from any country that they chose. This became more apparent when it comes to stock exchanges and with the trading of debts between countries. Now, not only goods are imported and exported, but also, the labor is also exported. Try calling a customer service representative for a company located in America; it is most likely that you will be speaking to someone from India, the Philippines or another country with an accent that might be difficult to understand.

There has long been a debate over the negative and positive effects that this economy has on the people involved in it. To start with, those who are pro globalization feel that it helps to spread the wealth so that all countries have a chance to succeed and prosper. Those who are against this kind of economy feel it is causing a lot of damage to our environment, and it brings about a great deal of costs to humans including poverty and unemployment.

What is known for certain is that this new kind of economy could set us all up for some form of a disaster. We are so connected it is hard to imagine getting things done without the help of at least one other country. We have to think of the worse case scenarios to see what could happen. What if one of the other countries that we rely on does start to fail? What if we weren't able to get the food, or natural resources that we use to make the food, for days, months or even years? How would this affect all of us?

It's these questions that scare a lot of people. Many people are worried that soon the system is going to breakdown, and everyone is going to be feeling the pinch.

What Happens When One Country Has a Bad Year?

With our global economy, we are all connected in one-way or another. We all depend on each other, no matter how big or small the other country might be. For example, if a smaller country failed, we wouldn't have the natural resources needed in order to run our machines and produce food or other products. If the bigger countries failed, the smaller ones would not be able to purchase some of the food and other products that they rely on. This system has a delicate balance where everyone needs to work together to benefit and flourish.

This situation illustrates what will happen if just one of the countries starts to fail. We are so connected that it is never good   if anyone, no matter the size, begins to fail. While the complete failure of one country is not necessarily going to have the same impact on all the other countries, the issue is going to be felt by some degree by everyone involved.

Let's take a look at an example. The debt crisis of Greece is a good example which demonstrates how countries are dependent on each other. While this situation was more a matter of money and the fact that Greece could not pay off debts owed to other countries, or to even support its own people, it does show how delicate a balance all of this is when it comes to a global economy.

The Greek Crisis

The collapse of the Greek economy is not something that happened overnight. It was a long, drawn-out process that had been brewing for many years and is still being played out at the time of this book being published. In this situation, the government of Greece was taking on more debt than it could handle. The government was considered corrupt, regarding this, because it was spending more than it should, knowing full well that it would never be able to pay off the debts.

Greece was first noticed, for this debt crisis, shortly after the issues with Wall Street in 2008. The global market was already crashing thanks to how financially poor America was doing at the time. Greece announced, during 2008, that it had been understating its deficits for years. Greece was considered one of the financial centers of Europe for many years, and then all of that came into question.

Because of this, many countries shut Greece out. It was not allowed to borrow using the financial markets. This just made things worse and by 2010, Greece was headed for bankruptcy, something that was certain to make things worse. No one would have believed this could ever happen but it was.

To try and avoid bankruptcy, the first of what would be two international bailouts for the country were issued. These were large sums of money that came out to about $264 billion for Greece. There were several conditions attached to this so-called "bailout." The lenders imposed some harsh terms that required high taxes on the people and deep cuts to the budget. The whole of the Greece economy needed to be changed as well to making it friendlier for business, meaning more tax income to pay off the loans.

The issues began early on for the Greek people. Even though the government was taking in a lot of money from loans through other countries, they were not paying it back. It was instead driving up the inflation rate for the Greek people. This worked well for a while because it allowed for more jobs and more money to be moved around in the country, but soon, the debtors came knocking and wanted their payments. The government had no way to repay those loans, which at that point, had accrued considerable interest. The money began to dry up as the government attempted to pay back what they owed. Simply, that did not work.

The Greek populace began to suffer. Their jobs dried up soon because the government was no longer stimulating the economy.

People were seeing more taxes placed on them in the hopes of being able to pay off the loans. But, when the majority of your paycheck is going to the government rather than to yourself, you are barely surviving, and nothing is left to live on. Purchases made at stores would be minimal and the taxes the government was able to secure were declining.

So at that point, Greece was pretty much stuck … unable to pay what they owed, no matter how hard the government tried. Their people were starving and unemployed and there just was no way that the government would be able to get money. The big question was what was going to happen next?

In the past, before all of this modernization, the problem would   be just between Greece and its creditors. Greece would have to find some way to pay back their debts and make things right, or the creditor would pretty much be in charge of Greece for a number of years. These are really the only two that would be involved. The creditor might lose a bit of buying power for a bit of time, but they could use some of the taxes and natural resources belonging to Greece to help them through the tough times.

But, in the modern world, this debt situation became a bit more confusing and certainly more complicated. Greece is not just connected to the creditor, but to the rest of Europe as well. Thanks to the whole of Europe being on the Euro system, this becomes even more complex. If Greece fails, all of Europe would see an economic down turn as well. This would bring the economy of all of Europe to a standstill due to the mistakes of one member nation.

With the bailout money, which was supposed to help the economy of Greece, Greece was still itself in trouble. Unfortunately, most of the bailout money went to their loans payments in an attempt to reduce stress and international pressure.

This meant that the money never got to the people of Greece. This was a bad cycle because the government would never be able to pay all their debts unless a recovery was successful.

But, that cannot happen without enough money to aid the rebuilding of the economy.

The issue surely got worse. The creditors wanted to get their money back as soon as possible to help their own economies. But, Greece just was not able to enable the plan to work. Their relationships with other countries became fragile, and soon things began to decline for many European countries.

If Greece failed, no one knew for certain how bad the situation would get for the creditors and for other countries that were helping.

What once should have been a simple transaction could have influenced all of Europe and, even worse, spread to most countries throughout the world.

How does this affect the rest of the world?

While this example talks more about finances between countries, the same thing can happen when it comes to food and other supplies. Let's say Greece, instead of having trouble with money, was having trouble with their wheat supply that the world depended on. For years, they had been wasting away the wheat and not taking good care of it. Soon, they run out of wheat and aren't able to trade it any longer. What are the other countries going to do?

Wheat is a staple for many countries, and you can find it everywhere. And, unless you are on a solely meat diet, you may find it really hard to make it by without wheat. This would have profound effects on everyone and would result in a lot of chaos, much like the financial crisis that occurred not too long ago.

The lesson: Now that we are a global economy, it is possible that everyone is going to start failing if just one country begins to fail. Greece is a country far away from us, one that most of us have never had much contact with, but because of some bad mistakes of their government, we might find ourselves in a financial crisis.

This can happen at any time, with any country, and could be devastating regardless the particular resource that is at risk.

Can We Survive On Our Own?

The next question that comes up is whether we would be able to survive on our own. Would the people of America be able to survive if there were a major collapse in the existing system with other countries?

There is sometimes two answers to this question which we need to take into consideration. First, the people of America would find it very difficult to get along as a self-sufficient player. Despite being a great big nation, we do rely heavily on other countries for many supplies. We import much of our food, clothing, gasoline, and other materials from other countries, even though some of the food we produce here is sent to other countries to be processed and packaged..

If there were a large supply-chain collapse from other countries, it would be hard for America to recover quickly. The processes just aren't in place to make this happen.

If the other countries collapsed, we would be struck with a lot of shortages. We would be out of food, clothing, and other supplies and there would be wide spread panic.

But, there is a ray of hope in this for America. We were once an isolationist country for many years and had everything we needed. If government were able to get everything in order, we could start producing our own needs again. We would be able to grow our own food and stop relying on others for everything. But this would require the right decisions from those on top, and it would take some time to implement.

In the meantime, we would all be stuck scrambling around and trying to find a way to survive. This is exactly why we need to prepare now.

You can't rely on others to make sure that you are safe; you especially should not rely on the government. The government and other "powers to be" believe that the global economy is the right system to help everyone grow and prosper. While this is something that can occur when the system is working properly, when the system stops working, we will find that everyone is going to fail to some degree.

This can scare a lot of people who see that many countries are having issues in this tough economy causing them to panic. Getting prepared ahead of time can ensure that you are ready and able to survive, even when everyone else is in panic and all the food supplies are gone.

As this chapter illustrated, the events of the world can affect America, even if we are not the ones directly involved. Because of the interconnectedness between countries, when one starts to fail, it can cause entire systemic problems for everyone. Being ready to survive for some time, in the case of a huge systemic collapse, can help to keep you safe.

CHAPTER 3:

How Governments Control Populations

Sometimes, a shortage in food has nothing to do with a country going through a famine or a natural disaster. Sometimes, the shortage is more *man-made* than anything else. These are most certainly worse than the natural causes. At least, with the natural causes you know when the weather clears up, you should be able to get the food supply back. But sometimes, the government is
the reason for the food shortage and for many reasons.

If you ask most people, they have a similar idea of what government should be providing. Government should be a body that works for the people and protect them, furthering their individual best interests and helping the people to live a better life. While this is a great plan, in theory, most of the time, this is not what happens with government. Most governments start out with great ideas and plans; but over the years, the governments become corrupt and begin acting in a way that allows them to   stay in power, and the ones in control tend to benefit more than the people they govern.

Don't believe this to be true? Take a look at the government that   is in place in America. The original founding fathers of this country were interested in life, liberty, and the pursuit of happiness. They wanted the people to have the ability to follow the American dream, and the whole was to have a government that represented the people. This was to be the totality of their duties, to be beneficial to the people and nothing else. But now, politicians think they deserve to be in power, take advantage of their power, and often jet off to expensive vacations, using tax dollars taken from the citizens. Many of the laws including "Obama Care" don't even apply to the members of the congress and senate. They live under different rules and can even vote themselves entitlements, including pay increases without ever getting approval from the people who elected them. The government has changed dramatically from what it was in the past, and it is easy to see that other governments might do the same.

One way that you might see a food shortage begin in your country is due to the government controlling the food supply chain. They accomplish this by taking all of the food that is being produced in the country and pretend there is no surplus, or by   not trading with other countries to get more food. There is the opportunity to give people more food, but selfishly they keep the food restricted, often for them. The motives behind this would be to control the   population.

Why would the government do this? There are several reasons that are explored in this chapter. The first one is that with less food, the population is going to stay small. If the government only hands out a limited amount of food to people and keeps telling their population that the food supplies are running low, then they are less likely to have more children for fear that parents won't be able to feed them. This lower population makes it easier for the government to remain in control. The second one is that the government is able to control the people by controlling the food. For example, if the government is worried about citizens revolting, they may consider taking away all food supplies. This makes the populace too weak to fight anything they feel is wrong. Plus, the government can then blame others as the culprits of the food shortages and redirect the anger away from them onto someone else.

There are many people who believe that most of the food shortages in the world have nothing to do with food scarcity.

They believe that the areas that are experiencing these food shortages are actually going through a period of depopulation at the hands of government. This whole idea of food shortage is to control the populace and make the population size decrease so they are less able to fight those in power. If you look at the history of counties where this has happened in the past, and then looked at the type of government which was in place, it makes it easier to see how this occurred.

This chapter will to explore all of these points and give you another reason why you must consider getting prepared in the event that there will be a food shortage in your area.

Less Food Equals Lower Population

This idea that the government is holding the power through food can be seen in America even now. In fact, it is believed that the American government was able to destroy at least 90% of the family farmers throughout the world, including in the United States, in order to have better control over people once the food supply was gone. Kissinger, the man who was the mastermind of a report on population control stated, that if you can control the food, you could control the people. And thanks to the American government, only six corporations that work on an international scale control the majority of food production in the whole world. You have to admit that this is very scary.

This information alone should be troubling to everyone: six companies being in control of all the food supply and grain reserves in the world! This is an incredibly small number when you realize that there are 196 recognized countries in the world and how many people rely on this food. Most of the countries are not being represented, and those who work for this large agribusiness basically control all the food. Make them angry or make them worried for their wealth and influence, and you might be the next who doesn't get food to eat.

Controlling the citizens of a country is one of the biggest tasks that a government must do. The government wants to be the sole voice in deciding what decisions are made, how others should react to those decisions, and a whole host of other things. But, if the people are able to rise up and overtake the government, and that could happen if they are well fed, feeling good, and their numbers are large enough; then, they could take control away from the politicos. The government does not want this to happen. They want to retain control. In the modern world, the American government, as well as others, are able to control their populations and populations of other countries to ensure consistency of political power.

This idea is called democratic unfreedom, (http://www.truth-out.org/news/item/9769-democratic-unfreedom-social-technique- and-the-manufacture-of-control) is supported with scientific rationalism. Those in charge are not just going to take away the food supply and wait for other do-gooder groups to come in and make the situation better. Instead, they are going to make it look like those who were impacted were the ones who caused the issue. When there is local famine, those in power are going to talk about how overpopulation of that area put a strain on the society and the land, and that is why they are having problems. This removes any sympathy that might occur in most cases.

This management and control of the food supplies has become a political and corporate priority for many years, and some large companies in the United States are the ones who are controlling the entire situation. According to Henry Kissinger, "Control oil and you control nations, control food and you control the people." This seems to still hold true, even today, for many governments and corporate officials who want to retain their power.

Do you want to be controlled by food shortages in your area? It is not just in foreign countries where this control is being utilized. It is only a matter of time until the governments in larger, first world, countries start to use their influence on the American people. This might already be in play, with the poor populations voting for particular candidates, because they are brainwashed to believe that the other side is trying to suppress them. Do you want to become a part of all this, or do you want to be able to have control and security for your family? This is why it is so important to prepare your survival supplies now.

This is not a game, so procrastination is not a wise option. Don't let the powers to be decide when you will eat, how much you will eat or if you will starve. Take matters into your own hands and start getting prepared long before crisis hits.

When Government Controls the Food, It Controls the People

To illustrate how a government is able to control its own population or, at least, the population of its enemy, with controlling food, let's take a look at the potato famine that occurred in Ireland long ago.

This is a well-known case in history that shows how famine changed the way a population interacted with those around them. During the 1840s, a famine started to hit Ireland. The main source of food in this area was potatoes and all of a sudden the people of the area couldn't grow potatoes. This potato crop failure was due to a late blight, a disease that destroyed both the leaves and the edible roots, or tubers, of the potato plant.

Since this was the main food staple, there were many who began to starve to death and many who survived left Ireland in hopes of going somewhere where food was available.

There are many people who don't believe this was something that occurred by chance. This idea is further developed by the idea that Lord John Russel, one of the leaders of the British government at the time, did nothing to help the Irish people and actually made matters much worse. All in all, this famine ended up killing about 1/8th of all Ireland's citizens. Many more left the country.

Some wonder how this potato famine got so bad so fast. In most modern famines, there is only one area that gets affected when it comes to a famine. It is usually not the whole country that would experience this situation simultaneously. Plus, this famine lasted for a long period of time, 1845 and 1852, which was very unusual.

Most famines will just last for a few years, but this one ended up lasting for seven consecutive years, never seeming to improve.

Even after the famine ended, there was still the issue of hunger throughout Ireland. The poor had become extremely dependent on the British and often they feared dying of starvation more than if they were evicted from their homes. Many scholars believe this fear was exactly what the British were trying to instill in the population.

Apparently, the British wanted to "break the spirit" of the Irish and, if that was their goal, it succeeded. Before the famine began, the Irish people were organizing a revolution against the British crown. They wanted to become their own country and be able to make their own decisions. But, the British wanted to hold on to Ireland and continue to rule it.

The potato famine was just what the British needed to create fear in the Irish about something more important than planning their revolution. The Irish discovered that it was really hard to fight against the British when they were starving and homeless. But, did the British really create that famine which is a part of history?

There will always be people that believe the British engineered this famine. History says that there was a blight that came to Ireland during this time that set it all off. But, the amount of grain that went into Ireland and Britain should have been sufficient to feed everyone. There was food, but most Irish were not getting this food, supposedly because it wasn't being distributed properly. But why, you might ask?

It is assumed that while British and Irish leaders brought enough food to bridge the gap that the potato famine cause, getting it distributed to the populace was not working. The potato blight was real thing. The British had nothing to do with causing the potato from disappearing. But, obviously, they took an opportunity control the Irish and prevent them from seceding from the British Crown and become their own country.

Instead of working to help the Irish, and providing them with grains they needed to stay healthy and strong, the British kept this food source for themselves, enabling them to control the Irish and stop possible revolution.

Because the British hid the grain supply from the Irish, they went without food, creating an artificial famine. Why would the British do this?

Most educated people believe it was to maintain control, or more likely crush the potential of revolution. The British didn't Ireland to be independent. And, the famine was the perfect situation for the Crown to capitalize on. If you believe that Britain wanted to stay in control, like so many others do, they deprived the Irish of food that would have saved them.

Since the Irish were busy trying to survive and keep their homes, they weren't able to manage developing an uprising for a long time. The British were successful in suppressing the Irish population in order to maintain the power.

So, the British did not cause the famine, but they viewed it as an opportunity. They used it to their advantage to control the Irish.

This is but one example of what might occur when a government or group decides to use food to control others. When you create a famine or control the food, you are effectively able to control populations. While you can't necessarily stop population growth completely, when people are worried about not being able to feed themselves, they are going to restrict their having more children.

This reduces populations permitting political leaders to remain powerful. It also makes people forget about political views when they can't even feed themselves.

Food Shortage vs. Depopulation By Local Government

There is a group of people who believe that the food crisis we are now facing is not something random. They don't believe the lies that the government is telling its citizens, such as the weather has been bad, a natural disaster is causing problems, or something else is really the truth. Many of these groups instead believe, the whole concept about food shortages is just a way to depopulate Earth. Governments want to slow down growth so that they can maintain control.

Sure the politicians will keep talking about how we are running out of food and other resources, and at some point, the Earth will be destroyed. But, is this the real story?

Often, this is enough to make people question how they care for the world, and to even consider having fewer children. When fewer children are born, depopulation is the result.

So, is there any truth in this? Are governments really working against their citizenry in the hopes of depopulating the world? Let's review a plan that was discovered in 1974 that indicates how the government would perform genocide through food   control.

Kissinger's 1974 Plan

The U.S. National Security council was busily at work during 1974 to lower populations. During that time, they had worked with Henry Kissinger to compile a study about population growth and how it would affect U.S. security. In this study, were reports, later proven false, that stated that a large population increase in other countries, especially third world countries, would bring a huge threat to the U.S. national security.

Even though the reports were full of falsehoods, this study became part of an official Presidential policy with President Ford in 1975. This study outlined a plan to reduce the population growth in all of these countries, mainly through birth control. But, since birth control isn't that effective, and relies on people actually using it correctly, the plan also outlined the use of famine and war to reduce population. These plans were utilized during following years, and many higher up in the American government utilized them to keep third world country populations   minimized.

Undoubtedly, the methods Kissinger introduced were not original. One of his sources was a report created by King George VI, in 1944, called the Royal Commission on Population. This report was very similar to Kissinger's as it considered the measures that the nation should take to keep itself safe.

This commission discovered that England was threatened by how much population growth the British colonies had. If the colonies had more people than England itself, it was highly likely that the colonies might rise up and want to secede. This would harm the interests, as well as the security, of England.

Kissinger was able to use many of the ideas found in the King George VI's plan to form his ideas and theories. Kissinger outlined how the population throughout those same colonies could cause issues for America as well. 13 countries were singled out in this report, and the United States needed to expend some extra energy utilizing the plan, according to Kissinger. These countries included Colombia, Brazil, Mexico, Ethiopia, Egypt, Nigeria, Turkey, the Philippines, Thailand, Indonesia, Pakistan, Bangladesh, and India.

The report also discussed how population growth found in these countries was really worrisome because the population could increase their strength and could pose a big threat to the United States besides their own country.

So, what actually took place thanks to this report? Kissinger enumerated some measures that he recommended to deal with the threat. First was birth control. Plus, there were other programs that would help reduce the population. By handing out birth control, it was less likely that the people would continue to have children and populate the country and thus it would reduce the populations.

It worked, at least to a certain degree. Previously, these countries had a higher percentage of unplanned pregnancies than other countries. By distributing birth control in these countries, unplanned pregnancies reduced considerably and it was easier to control the amount of new births. But, this was as effective as they had thought. Not everyone would voluntarily take birth control that they were given.

Just because you're given free birth control doesn't mean that you are going use it. If you wanted a family or had religious beliefs that kept you from using contraceptives, then it would not work because you wouldn't take it.

Kissinger took it a step further to ensure that the population decrease would occur. A second measure prevented some food supplies from reaching their destinations. First, Kissinger predicted that some places would undergo some famine. Whether this was due to something U.S. government was provoking, such as crop burning, or other causes, or because this was the time in history when famines were likely to occur is uncertain. But, there were famines across the major countries on Kissinger's list. Kissinger went further; he insisted that emergency rations not be given to these countries, despite their starving by this point.

Most people believe the famines were not a natural occurrence. In fact, looking through some records, it was demonstrated that during the 1970s, America started changing its policies towards these countries. They stopped U.S. investments in these listed countries for infrastructure and irrigation. The existing irrigation systems began to deteriorate without maintenance money or investments to build new water systems. This made it difficult to farm their land and farmers couldn't direct water to their crops. Soon the amount of food in production decreased and rationing began.

No matter how much propaganda existed that population growth was the true issue, it was actually the investors of that time, as well as the politicos in power, who determined the fate of those countries on Kissinger's list. It wouldn't have mattered if the population were halved at the time, those in power decided to cut off funding and any help that was needed to assist those on the list and prevent them from starving to death.

When people are desperate for food sources, it is near impossible for them to increase population. People who can't care for themselves with enough food will have trouble taking care for their children; they certainly will consider not having more children. This was another form of birth control. In fact, it worked much better than handing out birth control pills, plus it was effective in killing some of the people already alive. This loss of food was effective in decreasing population size in many areas of the world.

Due to pressure apply to populations in third world countries, a famine did occur and population decreased. This is when Kissinger, and his cronies, took it a step further. Instead of just being happy with their success, they started to discuss how it was the fault of those suffering for their famine and starvation.

If they hadn't populated so quickly, maybe their system would have been able to handle the extra burden. It was the people's fault for running out of food. This brought along sympathy to Kissinger's cause and made it easier for him to get his diabolical work done.

This was not solely a U.S. government plan that went into play. Several multinational corporations got into this game as well. For example, Richard Freeman wrote a summary in the Intelligence Review which stated how the elite were trying to put a tourniquet on the production of food as well as the export supplies. This was originally used in poor nations but is starting to move up to the more advanced countries as well. According to Freeman, this is possible because of the system of agribusiness, which is discussed a bit more in the next section.

Windsor's Global Food Cartel

While it may not be obvious to the average citizen, the food supply for the entire world is controlled mainly by 12 countries. While there are a couple dozen other countries that are satellites for the bigger companies, they all work together under a group that is known as Britain's House of Windsor.

Altogether, this cartel is the one that is in control of the grains and cereals for the whole world whether you are looking for rye, sorghum, barley, oats, corn, or wheat. In addition, they are also in charge of all the spices, sugar, vegetables, fruits, fats, oils, dairy, and meat. They pretty much control the food supply of the whole world when it is broken down.

It is believed that the tens of millions of people die because they aren't able to get enough food to eat, is the result of this Windsor group. This group is ruthless in holding on to the food and money that it already controls and it is ready, at a moment's notice, to apply the tourniquet to the supply food.

The sad part is, as more news of famine spreads and more people start to die of hunger, the quantity of food that Windsor is retaining is ever increasing.

The idea of using food as a weapon against the populace is not new, It's been around for almost four millennia. If you would review back to Babylonian history, you'd see how they used food to overpower their enemies. Imperial Rome also used this option with Venice, the Dutch, and many more civilizations.

This is not something new that governments and big corporations just thought up to use to make things easier and more profitable for them. Simply, history repeats itself.

Of course, these methods benefits those on top, but the ideas have been around for thousands of years. And today, instead of one group doing it against one enemy, this cartel is using their power against everyone they can.

The most powerful rulers in this world run the cartels. Anyone who dares to go against a cartel will experience financial loss. Obstructing what the cartel wants will cause the food supply to disappear and perhaps many people would starve to death. It is a gruesome idea, but it seems to match up with what is occurring in many parts of the world right now.

The third world countries that the United States listed in the original Kissinger report are struggling from lack of necessities and the population is being controlled through lack of food, funds, and support of any kind.

So why would the U.S. government want to do this? There are a few theories as to why. All the countries that were original outlined in the report present certain dangers to American safety, or have at some point in time caused trouble to the American people. Perhaps they put in a leader that the American leaders did not approve of, or perhaps the U.S. worried that these countries would become too powerful to manage. The U.S. government put these measures into place to protect the U.S. from a foreign power entering the arena and taking away the U.S. money and power through any economic means.

A second school of thought is that the American government wanted to use this method to reduce its own population down and third world countries were a testing ground. They surely demonstrated that the issues in these third world countries were extensive and discussed how overpopulation was to blame.

By discussing these concepts, the American government could demonstrate that if population continued to increase, in the U.S., at such an alarming rate the same problems would arise as they did in third world countries.

Did it work? The average household size in 1973 before Kissinger's report came out was 3.48 people per home. In 2014, the average household size had dwindled down to 3.13. While these numbers may not be a direct result of the report, it is likely that this information, as well as the effect of the U.S. media, had a lot of impact on how many children families chose to have in the years following 1974.

This is not something that just happens in third world countries or elsewhere. How long before the Windsor cartel, or our own leaders, decide that we are growing too quickly or opposing them? This could happen any day, and do you really want to be lacking in preparedness when it does occur? Getting your survival gear ready, and in place, is vital for when this occurs. It will save your families and your own life.

CHAPTER 4:

The Influence of China

Even without a food shortage, we need to be on the lookout. America has made many enemies throughout the years and there are countries who would enjoy nothing more than harming us. Many of the foods that we consume in America might be contaminated; even the foods that we produce within our country are often sent to other countries for processing and packaging.

Is it really safe to send our foods elsewhere? Shouldn't we, as a great nation, assure that our own food stays safe for our citizens? While most people don't think about what happens with their food before it reaches their tables, it can be a legitimate problem.

One country that has considerable control over our food is China. In fact, the majority of foods we consume in the U.S. is either grown in China, or we send the food over there for processing and packaging before it returns to the U.S. to be put on the supermarket shelves. Giving this much control over our food to China can backfire as people and animals have become sick.

It's a rather common belief that China is trying to poison the American people by tampering with the food that we consume. It would be fairly easy for the food processing companies in China to do this.

These food processing companies are empowered to produce much of the food that we consume. And, in some cases, for the food that we grow in the U.S., these companies handle the packaging of them before returning them to us. It would be very easy for Chinese companies to poison our entire country. Even if they aren't currently doing so, the fear of this even becoming a reality with people getting very sick before anyone notices has sent thousands of people to start stockpiling their own foods in preparation.

The situations gets further complicated when we send over our foods to another country for processing or packaging. While there are regulations in place through the Food and Drug Administration, there are also loopholes that make discovering who has actually handled our foods difficult to know.

Many products that don't go through a substantial transformation don't have to list any other country besides the country of origin, no matter where the food is sent to for processing.

For example, if peanuts are grown and harvested in the U.S., and then shipped in bulk to be roasted and packaged, China often will not appear on the label since it's still the same peanuts when shipped back to the states.

Because of these fuzzy rules, it because extremely difficult to determine what's safe to eat and what might have been tampered with. For those who worry that China is purposely trying to impact our food supply to poison us, these attempts of China to gain influence over America's food companies is troubling.

What Foods are Made in China?

You might be astounded to discover how many "American" foods don't come from the U.S. at all. Many of the brands we enjoy and serve on our tables actually come from China. This gives China a lot of control over our food and our health. Some of the products made in China and sold in America include:

- Europe's Best and Green Giant vegetables are all from China

- Garlic—China is considered one of the biggest producers for garlic throughout the world.

- Honey—unless you purchase the honey at a local farmers market, it probably comes from China.

- Our Family—this is a brand typically thought to be very American. But several of the products, including their mandarin oranges, come from China.

- Pears and peaches—while the food product may not come from China, the jars that hold the food are produced in China.

- Frozen fish products—most of these come from China. They are produced in fish farms, which have no regulations on them.

- Fruit cups—many of these are packaged in China.

- Apple juice—be careful of any apple juice you are consuming. China produces a lot of pesticides, which stay on the fruit and can get into your juice and make you sick.

- Processed mushrooms

US Food Companies That Belong to China

America is the country of opportunity. It is consider one of the best countries to be in to change your outlook on life, grow a business, and really see your dreams become a reality. This has been one of the main ideas associated with America for a very long time, but how much longer will this reality continue?

Even today, it is possible that China has started to take over many companies that are thought to be American. American companies offer the best opportunity to see growth in your portfolio, and they offer a chance for the people of China, including the government, to get their foot in the door. And this is not only in the food company sector. Chinese investors have placed great sums of money in American companies such as Oaktree Capital and Goldman Sachs.

As of 2010, it was believed that direct investment from the Chinese was over $6 billion, but many experts believed that the amount could be much higher because there are more direct means to invest that are not counted.

The Chinese have been slowly increasing their investments in America's food industry. One of the Chinese holdings is Smithfield Foods. This company is the head organizations of many popular food companies including:

- Healthy Ones
- Carando Classic Italian
- Curly's
- Margherita
- Kretschmar
- Nathan's
- Gwaltney
- John Morrell
- Cook's
- Armour

In 2008, China National Cereals, Oils, and Foodstuffs, Corp. began to invest in Smithfield Foods. At that time, they had invested sufficiently to own just under 5 % of the total holdings. The company was only worth about $122 million at the time. A few years later in 2013, Shuanghui International took over complete control over Smithfield foods and holds 100% of the shares. At this time, the company become worth over $7 billion.

Before 2008, Chinese companies did not hold significant investments in the food industry, although they had begun working on other industries such as financial, medical, and automotive.

Additionally, some of the cereals that we eat come from a company called Weetabix. Originally, Weetabix was founded in

Ontario, Canada and was associated by many to be from Canada. But in 2013, a company based out of China, called Bright Food, took over the Weetabix brand. Consumers, however, will not find this information on the box. The cereals still say "manufactured by The Weetabix Food Co. Ltd."

There are many food products with this issue. They may change ownership so a business is run by another country, without the consumer ever knowing. Loopholes in FDA regulations make it easy for foods to go between different countries without ever informing the consumer to this fact.

Chinese Food Making Us Sick?

At this point, you may be thinking, what's the big deal? Why should it matter that many Chinese companies are taking over our American food companies or helping out with food packaging? This is a capitalist society and with a global economy, it almost dictates that many different countries will work   together.

The issue is, many people, as well as animals are getting sick, especially on foods that come from China. Let's take a look at one example of food from China harming others.

In 2014, there was an outbreak of illness and death in dogs all over the U.S. From this case, it is believed that almost 5000 pet owners complained that their animals were getting sick from some jerky treats imported from China, and over 1000 dogs died after eating the treats. In addition, several people (two toddlers who got the treats by accident, and an adult who mistook them for another snack) became sick after eating these products as well.

The FDA has taken these instances very seriously, but after seven years of investigation and testing, they were not able to figure   out why the dogs, as well as humans, were getting ill. These   treats were the only ones to blame, all the pet owners affected had been using the same brand, but nothing was showing up in product besides the usual ingredients for dog jerky.

In about 60 percent of these cases, there were issues with liver disease and stomach aches. Another 30 percent included kidney disease, and the final 10 percent had other issues such as skin conditions. Of those who got the kidney disease, about 15 percent got a rare disease known as Fanconi syndrome.

One thing that has many pet owners worried about these treats is, that at one point, the FDA detected that there was traces of amantadine, an antiviral drug, which was found in some of the jerky samples from China about a year before these outbreaks. The FDA released a statement saying they don't think this is what caused the dogs to be sick, but most pet owners don't understand how this drug could be considered safe in the jerky treats.

Even though the FDA has stated these treats are safe for consumption and they do not attribute the consumption of these treats to the deaths, many veterinarians and pet owners disagree and feel that harsher measures need to be taken to keep animals and humans safe.

Where does the food contamination stop? These jerky treats had a major impact on dogs, and even some people were affected. How long before something gets slipped into other foods and can make humans sick as well?

This is just one example of how toxic food from China has affected the Americans. Many items from harmful honey and even melamine found in milk products are allowed to leave China, either intentionally or not, and many of these food products make it right into America since the government does not have strict food import inspections in place for the FDA.

It is important to be careful about the foods we are consuming. Even when the food label says made in America, there are many loopholes that allow food to be packaged or produced in other countries without the consumer knowing. Take the proper precautions with all your food and consider becoming more self- sufficient to stay safe.

CHAPTER 5:

It Gets Crazy When There Are Food Shortages

Food shortages are not something to mess around with. It is not going to take long until people realize the gravity of their situation. No one wants to think about starvation or what he or she will do when all the food is gone. They like being able to go to the supermarket and get all the supplies they need when it is convenient. But once a food shortage occurs, this convenience is gone.

When shortages occur, you are now fighting with thousands of people hoping to get the little bit of food left. What is worse, you have no idea when the food is going to come back. It could be in a few weeks or you may be on your own for years. This scary reality is what causes the rushes to the stores and the fighting that occurs after.

Things are going to go crazy when a food shortage is discovered, and people will start to panic. This would leave many people without the basic necessities they need to survive, and if you were not prepared you could be facing a bleak future.

A Story of a Family Trying to Survive During Food Shortage

Let's take a look at an example of what can happen when food shortages begin to impact a family.

You belong to the typical American family. You have two parents who both work hard, sharing the duties of working to pay bills, running the home, and taking care of the kids. You have two children who do well in school and keep you busy. You may have a little bit of savings and enjoy going on some vacations and hosting some big family gatherings in your home.

Like most American families, you feel like nothing will change your way of life. You like the modern conveniences and you couldn't imagine your life without being able to drive your car, get drinkable water out of the faucet, or run to the supermarket to grab groceries each week. This is a nice life many Americans enjoy, and outside of a few jars you canned from your vegetable garden last summer, you have nothing in terms of survival food prepared in case of an emergency.

Then the unthinkable happens. Famine, hurricane, dictator government, or some other event occurs. It cuts off your food supply. You hear the news about this event, about how you will no longer receive the food you count on to support your family. At first, you may think the news is a big hoax and wonder if anybody believes it. But, as the news continues to display this information, the harsh realization that life, as you know it, is gone settles over you.

Thoughts begin to rush through your head. What are you going to do? How will you be able to feed yourself and your family now that your major source of food is gone? You could grow a garden, but this is only going to last for a small amount of time and you will need to wait before any plant is mature enough to eat. Plus, you can only grow so many things in your garden and the rest of your diet will be sorely lacking.

Out of desperation, you and your spouse head to the supermarket, hoping to grab as many items as possible. The situation is even worse when you enter the doors. You see chaos all around. Others in your community have come to the same conclusion as you; the food supply will disappear soon and everyone will fend for themselves. You start to feel even more panicked and race around, grabbing as many items as possible. Often the prices are highly inflated.

It becomes a mad dash at the store. People you once considered your best friends will fight with you for any of the remaining food. Can you blame them? They have young kids to feed too and no idea when the situation will improve. Fighting breaks out in the aisles as people try to collect as much food as possible. While you wish you could go home and wait out the situation, you know leaving empty handed means your family is without food.

If you are lucky, you and your spouse may be able to get out of the store with a cart or two full of food that can last your family for a short time when added to the food already at home and you do some rationing. If you are unlucky, you may only get out with a few items and have to make due.

Back at home, you must reassess your situation. Things are looking pretty bleak and you worry about what will happen if the food shortage lasts for a long time.

During this, neighbors begin to turn against each other. You may start to lock your doors and windows and refuse to go out as often, worried about how the neighbors will react to you or try to cause you harm. You may understand that the neighbors aren't acting this way to be malicious; the stress, lack of food, and uncertainty of the future can cause people to react in different ways. But, it can still feel scary.

Your options are pretty limited at this point. There is very little chance the stores will get any new food during the shortage. If they do, there will be more fighting and danger at the stores. Some local farmers may still grow their food, as long as a natural disaster is not to blame for the food shortage, but the prices will skyrocket and you will again compete with others.

It is likely that you may not be working at this moment. The food industry employs a lot of people. You may be frightened to leave your home, and money will be tight.

You may start to consider growing your own garden or raising animals in your backyard. These are great ideas until the neighbors find out. Your neighbors want food just as much as you do, and once they see the produce of your garden or how yummy those chickens look, you can kiss your hard work goodbye unless you can find a way to hide these food sources in your home, you may go hungry.

In the best-case scenario, this shortage will only last a few weeks and you can stretch your food to last long enough. Once the food shortage ends, your family can go back to the supermarket and get your lives back to normal. But, what will you do if the food shortage extends after your food supplies are exhausted?

This makes the situation more frightening. People begin to look for an answer. If the food shortage is caused by a natural disaster, people turn to those in charge, like the government, to figure out why the situation has not resolved itself. Why hasn't the government sent in help to fix the disaster area and brought in food to feed the citizens? If a famine is to blame, why hasn't the government stepped in and found ways to trade with other countries to keep the people fed?

In some cases, people who are starving and searching frantically for food will look to their government officials for help, and find nothing. Instead, they see officials eating until they are stuffed   and having large parties without caring about constituents. When the people bring about their grievances, the government does   not seem to care about this suffering. This is the start of many revolutions that changed the course of history.

If you don't think this is true, what would you do to prevent your family from starving? How far would you go to ensure you and your family could survive, especially if you saw a solution to a problem or someone abusing the situation?

You need to prepare for this situation. No family should go without the basic necessities of food and water because of a natural disaster or a corrupt government. When you plan ahead and keep a steady food supply available, you don't have to worry. You don't have to go to the store and fight with others or worry about how long your family can last. Being prepared is good for you and your whole family when it comes to surviving.

Example of Food Shortages Causing Civil Unrest

The situation I mentioned looks pretty bleak. People will go to any lengths to keep themselves and their families safe and to prevent starvation. They will do things that under normal circumstances would never cross their minds.

In modern times, people don't believe these situations still occur. They may read about people starving in books, or see them in movies, and figure this is all fiction or something that only happened in the past. But in reality, food shortages are just as likely to happen today as they did in the past. Many revolutions and other civil unrest situations have occurred because people were hungry and wanted to feed their families.

Russian Revolutions

During 1917, there were two different revolutions that took Russia by storm. The result of these revolutions was the end of imperial rule in Russia and the start of events, which formed the Soviet Union. In March of 1917, the civil unrest grew into a huge revolt; helped along by the fact that many of the people were starving while the monarchy tried to maintain its tight controls. This revolt led to the final Russian czar, Nicholas II, to abdicate his throne.

The people at that time were not happy with the royals. Russia had faced some hard years and many were starving. Situations did not get better after World War I; it left the people struggling even more. By that time, the citizens of Russia had lost all faith in their leader and felt he should no longer be in charge. Nicholas was the catalyst to the revolution because of the way he acted against his own people. While they starved, he hosted grand parties and raised taxes to support his lavish lifestyle. Though agreeing to implement a Parliament to satisfy the people, any   time this Parliament went against his wishes, the Czar dissolved it.

In addition to these issues, the people of Russia were dealing with an economy that was going backwards during a time when many other countries were growing. Government corruption was everywhere; if a government official saw a chance to lie, cheat or steal from another person, they would do it.

All of these are the background to the start of the revolution, which began in February of 1917. The first phase of this revolution began during Russia's involvement in the First World War. Czar Nicholas believed he was the supreme power and the Russians needed to fight along with the allies to defeat Germany. This plan did not go well for Russia; their military didn't stand a chance against Germany and Russia sustained casualties never seen in any previous war. The war was expensive and drove the Russian economy even further into a black hole.

Starving, poor, and with no positive outlook for the future, the Russian people decided to revolt. The first order of business was to get rid of the Czar, whom many believed was the root of all their issues. At the very least, they believed he was doing nothing to further their interests to keep them from starving.

The first part of this revolution began during February of 1917. Demonstrators took to the street in St. Petersburg yelling and begging for bread. These demonstrators were soon met with workers from all over who had gone on strike. The police soon   got involved, but the protestors continued to air their grievances on the street. A few days later, with tensions high, the protestors began to destroy police stations.

Factory owners at this time were not happy. All their workers were on strike and not producing goods, no money was being made. The government formed a group called the Petrograd Soviet who were charged with stopping the uprising. Regiments of this group opened fire and killed demonstrators, but this was not enough to quell the spirit of the people, who were tired of living without food and having to work for almost nothing.

On this same day, the Czar again got rid of the Russian Parliament, a group that was supposed to protect the people, then tensions grew higher.

Just four days after it began, the revolution triumphed. Many regiments of the Petrograd Soviet defected to the side of the people and soon the government stood alone. After this time, the government was forced to resign. Nicholas handed over the throne on March 15, to his brother Michael, but Michael refused to take the crown. Effectively that ended the long reign of czars who had controlled Russia.

The fall of the imperial government resulted in a change for the country. For a time, the Petrograd Soviet and the provisional government worked together for a time. A few months later, during November of 1917, the Bolsheviks, led by Vladimir Lenin, took over the provisional government and they formed a new government to rule over the people, with them in control. They continued to rule the country until 1920 when the Union of Soviet Socialist Republics established itself as the rule of the land.

The rule of the Czars had been around for many years. Nicholas' family had held power hundreds of years and was once beloved by the Russian people. But once Nicholas began improperly controlling the government and people began to starve, he lost their support and love, which had been around for so long.

In just a few short years, Nicholas was taken from his throne and the anger of the people resulted in his whole family being killed. Starvation is a powerful motivator that causes the tides to turn quickly and governments to fall.

It would not take long for the same circumstances to arise in modern countries, and war, fighting, and death could happen all around us.

The French Revolution

The French Revolution is considered one of the bloodiest battles in modern history. It started during 1789 and did not end until Napoleon Bonaparte took over at the end of 1790s. During this time, the citizens of France redesigned their political landscape, effectively getting rid of all the old institutions, including the monarchy that oppressed them for so many years.

Before this revolution began, the French had become involved in the American Revolution, a move that proved costly to the country. In addition, King Louis XVI showed little regard for his people and was known to spend lavishly. These two events left the country nearly bankrupt.

While this issue is enough to cause civil unrest, the harvests in France had been poor for over twenty years. Bread prices skyrocketed, cattle suffered from disease, drought, and poor harvests of cereal products made the peasants and urban poor feel anger towards their King.

Feeling that they were underrepresented in the voting party at this time, the non-aristocratic people felt that they would never be heard. The nobles didn't want to give up their privileges and continued to overspend, regardless that their own people were starving.

The Estates-General came up with an idea to bring together the three orders of the voting populace at this time. The point was to get them to talk and perhaps bring peace. This did not happen; instead, the non-aristocratic members felt that they could be too easily outvoted by the other two orders and if the aristocrats had their way, the majority of people in France would starve to death.

Soon, this all exploded into a war against the aristocrats. But unlike the American Revolution, which was used as the symbol for the French, the people of France were not well organized. There was no clear leader in place to organize the troops. Most fighting occurred on the streets, unorganized, and casualties were massive for the French peasants.

Soon, the National Assembly came together hoping to make up a constitution, but things got even worse from there. This group decided to declare war against Prussia and Austria, two of the biggest countries in Europe at that time. The National Assembly believed some emigrants from this area were trying to build up troops to harm the revolutionists' goals.

In 1792, this group attacked the monarchy in Paris and then arrested the King. Following this, there was a massive killing of anyone who was not against the monarchy and would not join with the revolutionists. This got bloody really quickly, and soon the National Convention took over.

This group got rid of the monarchy and was able to effectively establish the French Republic. The King was killed early in 1793, and three months later, the Queen was killed as well.

Once the monarchy was gone, there was fighting amongst the revolutionists. Through these years, different factions had risen up, and now all of them were trying to take over. In June of 1793, The Jacobins took over the National Convention and started implementing radical measures such as a new calendar and getting rid of Christianity in the country. This was also the beginning of the Reign of Terror where anyone suspected of being against the revolution would be killed without a trial and for any reason.

This bloody time was finally ended in 1795 when the army, led by Napoleon Bonaparte, took up a new regime in France. All of those who were against this regime were silenced quickly and soon Napoleon successfully took over as an Emperor.

The events of the French Revolution quickly went out of hand. The people were tired of the bad crops, drought, and disease that pretty much made it impossible to have food to survive. Unlike some other wars that were more organized, though, those on the same side quickly turned against each other, and no one was safe in France for some time.

Food Riots in Modern Times

Food shortages are the main causes of civil unrest. People want to blame someone for their discomfort and starvation, and often the government is blamed. Even if government is not directly withholding the food, people believe the government should step in to help their people. Even though this is a historical problem, there are many instances in modern times where civil unrest occurs.

The Global Food Crisis in 2008 saw many food riots all over the world. While food was still available, prices reached all-time highs, making it difficult for people with a stagnant wage to afford food to feed their families.

The same thing is happening again. In 2014, the prices of food rose 4 percent internationally; this rise of food is similar to what occurred during 2008 and was the main cause of riots throughout the world. Concerned governments worry this might result in more riots and overthrown governments since the food shortages occur in such a short period of time.

The World Bank developed a definition to help governments in all countries to successfully recognize when a food riot occurs. According to the World Bank, a food riot is "a violent, collective unrest leading to a loss of control, bodily harm, or damage to property." The World Bank developed this definition in order to determine which food riots in the past would be cause for concern. Based on this definition, 51 riots, occurring in 37 countries, occurred in the 7 years between 2007 and 2014.

There is also some concern about what causes a food riot. The rising food prices was not the only reason that people in so many countries started to riot. For example, one of the food riots which is on record occurred in Vietnam was a result of decreasing prices. These prices occurred with coffee, the main export in Vietnam, which resulted in the average worker making less for the same amount of work.

In modern food shortages, there are two major types of food riots. During the first kind, the riots will show action against a government. This can be shown in public protests directly to the government or near government buildings. These often occur because food is all gone or because the price of food has become really high. This is the most recognized form of food rioting and will be reported by the media due to how much they affect other countries.

During the second type of food riot, the rioters will demonstrate near a specific food supplier. They may attack refugee camps, stores, and supply trucks. These will focus more on a local area and will occur most often when there is a huge decrease in the food supply.

These food riots are more common today than in the past. Due to the increased reliance between countries throughout the world, it is more likely that the failure of one will impact the others and cause food shortages in more than one country. In a world where the government is supposed to protect its people, the citizens are not likely to tolerate unnecessary food shortages and the possibility of starvation as they did in the past, resulting in more riots than ever before.

CHAPTER 6:

Could You Starve During a Natural Disaster?

Even if your government is not controlling the food supply, there are times when you may go through a food shortage. One of the most common reasons is a natural disaster.

There are many natural disasters which may strike at any time. Anything from a tornado, blizzard, hurricane, or extreme heat can cause damage to the food supply. When farmers aren't able to grow a specific kind of food because of a natural disaster, it becomes difficult for the rest of the world to get this food.

Most of these natural disasters are unexpected. They can wipe out whole regions and depending on the severity, could make it impossible to grow anything in that area for many years. Those living in the area will be hit the worst. They will go without food, shelter, and many basic necessities. Without a home to go back to, and often without any support, they are lost and have to either suffer or find somewhere else to start over. There is little chance; at least for a few months that food production will be resolved.

The rest of the world can feel the disaster too, although there are often other options to go with so the situation is not as dire. Depending on the food source destroyed, you may not even notice a particular natural disaster. But if the world's major producer or wheat is affected or another major food source, the rest of the world may have to go without that food source for a long time. This can make things bleak, and being prepared is the best option possible.

Natural Disasters Strike at Many Food Supplies

In many cases, a natural disaster is enough to disrupt the food supply from a particular area. The farms will lose all their crops they were able to grow up to that point and in some cases, the land will not be ready to grow anything new for a couple of years.

One case of natural disaster that shows this point well is a hurricane. During a hurricane, huge winds are able to create a big tropical storm usually in the form of big waves and water being dispersed in new places. Some hurricanes will occur far enough out in the ocean that no one is affected. Other times, the winds may be strong enough that the storm will reach land.

When the hurricane reaches land, disaster is everywhere. Homes are destroyed, water can strand people on the roads and they drown, and everything is covered with water. This water usually does not disappear in just a few hours after the storm. In fact, without proper precautions, this water may remain for a number of years.

Hurricanes are split up into five categories based on the storm's strength and how much damage occurs. These categories include:

- Category 1—these can get wind speeds up to 95 miles per hour. The damage is usually pretty small and often food supplies will not be interrupted.

- Category 2—these can get wind speeds up to 110 miles per hour. The damage is a bit more, but it usually isn't too bad.

- Category 3—these hurricanes can see wind speeds up to 130 miles per hour. This is when the damage starts to show up. Roofs and trees can become damaged and water will get everywhere.

- Category 4 - these hurricanes have been known to cause deaths and there is often extreme damage to the trees and buildings in the path of the storm. These winds can get up to 155 miles per hour.

- Category 5 - as the worst hurricane type, these can see winds above 155 miles per hour. Death is common for those who don't get out of the way and pretty much everything is destroyed during this storm. Food supplies often won't come back for a number of years while people try to rebuild their lives.

While category 5 is the worst, food supplies can be halted as a result of the smaller storms. These storms include a lot of strong winds and water damage that is far reaching. Many farms can lose all their crops and if the water stays in the way, it may be some time before the land is ready to be used again.

The people affected by the hurricane will need some time to reorganize. Some may look at the destruction and leave, assuming it will take too long to get things running again. Those who stay have a long road ahead of them. They need to work hard to get their land usable again and all too often they will need to spend time fixing the damage to their homes without having money or work.

In most cases, it can take years before the land is again workable as a result of one of the larger hurricanes. Those who relied on the food from these areas will either need to go without or find source to get these foods. The storm may have only lasted a few hours or a few days, but the impact will go on for many years.

This is true no matter which natural disaster is to blame. People lose property and lives during a natural disaster and getting things back to normal can take a long time. It is up to you to take control of your own food supply now, so you won't be at the mercy of a natural disaster taking away some of your necessities.

The Government is Not Prepared

While natural disasters are common, often governments are not prepared to take on the huge relief efforts needed to get the impacted areas back on track quickly. This can add years to the time it takes a region to repair the damages and perhaps get the food supply back up and running.

Many people see America as one of the biggest and best countries in the world, but even this country has trouble keeping up with natural disasters within their own borders. If America is not able to keep up with all the disasters, with all their advanced technology, how are some of the less economically stable countries supposed to keep the world's food supply safe?

Hurricane Katrina

One of the biggest disasters modern-day America has seen was Hurricane Katrina. This disaster occurred in 2005 and you can still see the impact over ten years later in the gulf coast area of Louisiana, Alabama, Texas, etc. 1833 people died in this disaster and the water damage ended up destroying many homes and businesses in just a few hours.

But, one of the biggest concerns at that time was how poorly the government responded to this disaster and how much more could have been done to help the people in there.

Before Hurricane Katrina, there had been some plans to prepare New Orleans in case of a huge natural disaster. In 2002, Joe Allbaugh, the FEMA director at the time, had determined that it would be easy for a large scale hurricane to reach the large city of New Orleans. After looking at all possible scenarios, FEMA conducted a drill called Hurricane Pam in 2004. This drill was meant to help responders take action in a situation where the storm completely destroyed New Orleans.

This drill showed that there were some pieces lacking in the response scenario to a potential major storm. This is why the government started to create more safeguards to try and protect this city.

The next year, there were reports that a large hurricane was making its way to New Orleans. Before the storm made it to land, Katherine Babineaux Blanco, the governor of the area, declared that Louisiana was in a state of emergency and then asked President Bush to declare the same, something that the President was more than willing to comply with.

Once the President declared this area in a state of emergency, FEMA was authorized to organize and them mobilize their resources to help out the residents who would be most affected by the storm. Before the storm hit land, a mandatory evacuation of the city was called for. For those who weren't able to leave the city, the superdome was opened to keep them safe on August 28, a day before this storm hit New Orleans.

Everything was in place to keep the city safe. While not everyone heeded the evacuation orders to leave the city, many had left to stay safe and many others went into the superdome to get away from the storm. A state of emergency had been declared and the proper aid was disbursed to keep things under control.

But if everything was in place, why was Hurricane Katrina such a devastating disaster?

The first issue came with FEMA's refusal to work with other agencies to control the impact of the disaster. The day of the hurricane, FEMA sent in 1000 workers to help provide some assistance to the city. To try and keep organized, FEMA asked that ambulance and firefighter crews not respond to any calls in areas that were hit by the hurricane unless they were contacted by state authorities. Because of this, many of those in need were left without emergency assistance since it took a long time to contact the state and then contact the emergency crews.

Some people felt that FEMA and the government wanted to take all the glory for this disaster. FEMA did not allow other emergency crews to come into the area. For example, the Red Cross was barred from coming into the area to help out those who needed urgent medical care, food, and clothing. The space in the superdome quickly reached capacity and situation soon became so bad, that it needed to be cleared out by August 31.

Over time, it became obvious that the government was not really prepared to take on the emergency. They claimed to never have received the information about how devastating this hurricane had become. While there were a lot of aid workers in the disaster area, the hurricane's effects continued on for many weeks after.

There were a lot of people willing to help with this emergency, but FEMA refused. The Red Cross wasn't allowed to help out. Firefighters and other emergency personal from across the state offered to help, but instead of being sent in to rescue citizens, they were made to hand out FEMA approved printed brochures. Nothing was organized and a disaster that many had prepared for became a catastrophe.

The government, even though they partially-prepared for the disaster, did a poor job of taking care of the people and the disaster caused a major catastrophe. The Army Corps of Engineers warned how bad it would be, and advance planned to rebuild a sea wall to prevent major flooding, but the funding was removed by the Bush administration and was used for the war in Iraq instead of protecting Americans in the poor sections of Louisiana.

Still, even though FEMA did a horrible job of coordinating efforts, this is more than what other countries can do. Many third world countries barely have a government, much less one to send in troops and supplies to help when a natural disaster occurs. When a situation like this occurs around the world, many more lives, as well as land and resources, can be lost.

Other Examples

There are examples of this kind of government inadequacy all throughout the world. The hurricane of 2005 in Pakistan resulted in thousands of deaths. These deaths are blamed on the poor construction of many buildings and people were not happy that government regulations were in place.

Often the response of a government will determine how bad the disaster strikes the people. When the government keeps an eye on the situation and sends in assistance right when the disaster strikes, the damage can be limited and the people will get back on track quickly. But, if the government is slow to respond, or doesn't respond at all, more people will be harmed and it takes much longer for the area to recover.

In some cases, outside aid determines how quickly the country will recover from their losses. In the example of the 2005 hurricane from Pakistan, the government was not quick to respond to the disaster, but aid from the United States and other humanitarian groups helped the people of Pakistan get back on their feet much faster.

The people who live in a country often rely on their government to keep them safe. When this doesn't happen, the damage becomes worsened and the residents find it is difficult to fix their homes, clear out the area, or even find their own food to survive. The food supplies regions impacted by natural disasters will come to a halt no matter what. But, it severely worsened if the government and other aid is not able or willing to help out the residents.

CHAPTER 7:

Food Storage Isn't a Fad

Never fall into the trap of thinking that a disaster can't happen to you. A disaster can happen to anyone and can leave a lasting impact that may never be overcome. Unfortunately, most people believe they are fine, their government will protect them, or there is plenty of food stored up to keep them safe. They may not understand the gravity of the situation, or they simply choose to ignore all the signs around them.

The idea of food storage is not a fad. While this may seem like a newer idea because of all the attention the prepper movement is receiving, the idea of food storage and being prepared for disaster has been around for hundreds of years. Your grandparents stored food in preparation for the Cold War against the Soviet Union. Before that, food storage was used to keep food safe while traveling on the Oregon Trail or to help people survive through the winter. This is not a fad you should ignore; instead, it is a lesson throughout all history that is capable of keeping you safe.

Our Grandparents Stored Food in Bomb Shelters

Even after the end of World War II, there were some high tensions between the major powers in the world. This period, known as the Cold War, brought to head some huge tensions between America and the then Soviet Union. The United States felt that the development of atomic weapons by the Soviets was a huge threat to their security, democracy, and to world peace. The residents of the United States felt something must be done to protect them and many feared an atomic attack for a long time.

Because of the fear many citizens had, the government created the Federal Civil Defense Administration. The main job of this board was to teach the American public how to prepare in case the Soviet Union decided to use their atomic weaponry against the United States. This information was distributed to all households in the country, especially those who lived in suburban area.

One way that many American people prepared for a potential attack by the Soviets was to create fallout shelters. In their most basic form, these shelters were concrete bunkers that contained some shielding to reduce exposure to gamma-rays. In most cases, the fallout shelter would be built using concrete, usually 12 inches or more thick. There would also be a thicker level of gamma-ray protector on the outside.

For families who had one of these fallout shelters, the area was placed either in their basement or in their backyard. In some instances, communities would come together and create a larger shelter to hold more people. The idea of these shelters was to protect the people inside from an attack and allow them to have a place to stay until the nuclear fallout dispersed.

Since people were expected to be inside these fallout shelters for a longer period of time, coming out could potentially cause harm due to the radiation. So, it was important to keep food supplies and water within the shelter. Each family was responsible for holding enough food inside their shelter to keep themselves and their families fed for quite some time.

Families interested in staying safe through an atomic bomb attack went to work creating storage foods, similar to the foods you would choose for a food shortage, to keep them fed until it was safe to come out. They would need to take it a step further, though, they were not able to create gardens or even hunt due to being confined in their small space, making it more difficult to replenish if something ran out.

Fallout shelters were built to have plenty of room for food storage. Many types of food must be created including canned goods, freeze-dried, dehydrated, and anything that would keep the food safe. While people knew about the impending doom, the exact date of attack was unknown so food needed to stay safe for a number of years.

This is a good example from the past where a threat to the lives of the American people was real. People worried they would need to spend a lot of time underground, without the possibility of coming back out for food, water, or other needs. They had to be prepared in advance, or they risked being caught in the attack or dying from the residual radiation.

While this atomic attack never happened, we can learn from our ancestors of the importance of always being prepared. We never will know when an attack will come, destroying our way of life we have come to know and love. Never make the assumption that everything is fine and no disaster will ever impact your life. The threats around our country and our food supply are even more prevalent today than before. So what are doing to survive? What will you do?

What Happens at the Grocery When Disaster Strikes?

Many Americans feel that disaster will never happen to them. They are comforted by believing this country is one of the largest and most developed in the world. But, food storage is just as important in this country as in any other. In fact, you should be more worried about the food disappearing here. The authors of the fateful 1974 Kissinger report of depopulation reside and even rule in this nation. What are you going to do when that disaster finally turns inward and you are without food?

Never assume food will always be available. Within minutes of a terrorist attack, food shortage, or natural disaster, there will be a mad dash to the supermarket, grocery, and convenience stores. Everyone is going to be in a panic and want to buy as much food as possible before everything is gone from the shelves. Without following in the footsteps of your grandparents, you may be left without some of your basic necessities.

Once disaster strikes, it won't be long before the stores have   been depleted of all your favorite foods, and have no food left at all. Everyone will descend upon the stores and it is unlikely that anything will be left by the morning after a crisis. Once the shelves are all bare? You will be responsible for your own food, for fighting against others who are just as desperate as you, and hoping to survive the situation.

Don't leave your fate up to chance. Take the time to prepare for a food shortage. Just a little bit at a time can add up over the years. And really, the disaster could happen today or it could happen in ten years. But adding a few extra items to the cart each month can add up quickly and in ten years, it will all pay off by keeping your family fed and happy in case of disaster.

CHAPTER 8:

The Ultimate Link - Terrorism and Our Food Supplies

Terrorism is a word that Americans, as well as other western countries, have become very familiar with. They hear about it in the media every day. But most people have no idea what terrorism really is and why they need to feel some concern about it.

Terrorism is not only frightening to our safety and well-being, but it could have some dire effects on our food supplies depending on where the acts occur.

According to the United States Federal Bureau of Investigation, there are a few different definitions of terrorism that are recognized. The first kind is international terrorism. In order for an activity to be considered international terrorism, there are three characteristics that must be met including:

- Violent acts or an act that is dangerous to the life of humans. The activity must also violate a state or federal law.

- Appearance of trying to coerce or intimidate the general population, to try and influence the policies of   the government using coercion or intimidation, or to affect the conduct of a government by kidnapping, assassination, or mass destruction.

- The activity occurs mostly outside America's territorial jurisdiction or transcends boundaries regarding the means of accomplishments.

The FBI also recognizes domestic terrorism. This is similar to international terrorism, except that the acts occur in an area that is under the territorial jurisdiction of the United States. This often makes it easier for the United States government to take control and apprehend the terrorists.

There are many criminal acts that you will hear about, but not all of them will constitute an act of terrorism. For the activity to be considered a "federal crime of terrorism" the act must be one that:

- Is meant to affect or influence the conduct or a government using coercion or intimidation or the activity must be a retaliation against the conduct of the government.

- Is considered a violation of at least one statute including killing or trying to kill using dangerous weapons on a federal facility or on employees or officers of the United States.

Not only does terrorism bring about a lot of fear, confusion, and destruction to a country, it also has the potential to cut off the food supplies of certain areas.

Even though the citizens of one country will be affected the most, the food shortage could become more far-reaching and start to affect other countries who need the food as well.

How Terrorism Impacts a Country

The effects of terrorism are far reaching and long-lasting. The act of terrorism, whether big or small, can have implications that will lasts for years, even after the mess is cleaned up and people try to move on with their lives.

Take a look at the attack on the World Trade Centers. At the time of this book's publication, this attack was over 14 years old. While most people have moved on and may only think about the fateful attacks once a year, there are many parts of their lives that are still affected by these attacks.

Think about the last time you were at the airport? This probably took a long time to get through the lines and you may have to go through security checkpoints several times to get to your plane.

Have you tried to get a passport recently? This often includes an extensive background check and can take weeks to get it in even if you have a clean record. While you may not think about this attack day-to-day, it still has an impact on your life.

No matter which country has went through an act of terrorism; there are affects that will change the rules of a country and even how it is governed. Some of the impact that terrorism can have on a country includes:

Economic

One impact that terrorism has on a country is economic. Many acts of terrorism will attack things that can ruin an economy. If the terrorists go after food, the country won't be able to trade with other countries. If the people are scared of leaving their homes, more may skip out on work and many won't go out shopping. Sometimes terrorists will threaten one country with harm if they continue trade with another; often the original country will stop trading to keep safe, and the economies of both will suffer.

Food supplies

In some terrorist attacks, food supplies can be harmed. The terrorists might take over all the food supplies in a particular country; then, the people aren't able to get everything they need. The terrorists might contaminate the food supply of a country, making the food unsafe to eat. The terrorists can control where food is shipped between countries, so neither one nor both countries are unable to get enough food to survive.

Controlling the food supply of a country is one of the most effective ways to get terrorists' demands met. People can be stubborn and will hold out against many things. But, most will not last long when they are starving; and, they will wonder how long before they get food to eat. When people worry about dying or see their children dying from starvation, they are more likely to give into the demands, even of terrorists.

Future laws

In many times, the future laws of a country impacted by terrorism is going to change. The government will implement laws that will make it difficult for future acts of terrorism to occur. You will find examples of this with the domestic and international flight laws.

Before 9/11, you rarely had to go through security checks and family and friends could walk with you to the door of the plane. Now, you have to go through at least one or two security checks per flight and your ride has to drop you off far away from the departure gate.

Laws with trading, traveling through a country, and who the country interacts with can change as well. The way that a government reacts to terrorism, and how well the new laws work, can often influence whether the people begin to feel safe again or if they will look for other alternatives to stay safe.

Fear of the people

The activity of terrorism is meant to place fear into the hearts of a group of people. This fear is calculated to force people to act in a certain way that benefits the terrorist. This fear is not something the people feel for a few hours; the fear is long-lasting, it is designed to last for quite some time so the population stays in line and don't attempt to go against the wishes of the terrorists.

This fear is going to change the way that people conduct their business. They may stop trading with a country that is associated with terrorists or change their rules to stay in line with what the terrorists demand.

Change of government

In some cases, there is a change of government due to terrorist acts. In one scenario, the group performing the terrorist acts is able to overtake the government and keep the rest of the country in fear. They will change the rules to meet their ideals and most people will stay in line for fear of what can happen.

In other cases, the terrorists may not take over the government, but there are still changes made to the ruling party. Citizens of a country may be upset with the way their government is handling the terrorists and will vote in new officials who can resolve issues. This can results in some new laws and actions that will keep the citizens safe and put the terrorists back in their place.

America: Cut Off From Food Supply

Creating a huge disaster, like the one found in 9/11, takes a lot of planning and time. A lot of people are involved and the huge casualties puts the whole country on alert for another attack. While many terrorists are more than happy to help out with these attacks, there is a more efficient way. These attacks might kill a few hundred or a few thousands of people, but when you get onto the food supply of a country, you can destroy hundreds of thousands of people with only a fraction of the effort.

After the terrorist attacks in 2001, many people started to worry that the next terrorist attack will be in the form of deliberate contamination of the food supply in this country. There are a lot of foods that are susceptible to being contaminated and the affects that come with this kind of attack can have huge implications on the whole society.

Everyone has to eat, and other those people who choose to make their own food and live on their own, everyone gets their food from the same sources. This means that if terrorists tried to get into the food and water of America, it would be far-reaching and could potentially a major part of the population before anyone notices what's happened.

The food industry in America has started to join with policy makers to determine the best way to keep the American food supply safe from this threat. This is one of the highest priorities in the country right now, but how effective can the government and the food industry be?

We discussed above how many of our foods come from different parts of the world. Food is imported here to give us more variety and to stimulate the global economy. Even some of the food we produce in America is sent overseas for packaging. The FDA states they perform vigorous checks on all food that comes back into the country, but research has shown that over 2/3 of the imported food is never checked.

Despite what we are being told about the safety of our food, it is increasingly easy for terrorists to get their hands on our food and place contaminants inside. These terrorists don't even need to be in America to do this. They can be in almost any other country to accomplish this, making it very difficult to track the culprit.

While many American citizens feel that their food is currently safe from terrorist attacks, there have been these attacks in the past. Back in 1984, there were some members of a religious commune in Oregon, who attempted to change the results of a local election. These members went to salad bars in the town and introduced the virus salmonella to make the voters sick. Luckily, no one ended up dying from the attack, but more than 750 people in the area got seriously ill.

There are many groups who believe some of the food borne illnesses as well as the diseases to livestock, such as mad cow disease, are a result of terrorists. But, since it is hard to determine whether these are natural events or terrorist attacks, they are not usually classified as acts of terrorism.

In addition, there is the possibility that terrorism in another country may affect our American food supply. If another country goes through a major terrorism attack or terrorists takeover the food supply in in another country, no one else is going to be able to receive this food. If this happens to one or two major trading centers, Americans could see their food supply dwindle rapidly.

Other Countries with Food Supplies Impacted by Terrorism

America is not the only country affected by conflict and terrorism. This is an event occurring all across the world. One example of this issue occurred in 2014 in Iraq.

Officials with the U.N. are currently concerned because millions of people throughout Iraq are most likely going to face food shortages due to the fighting throughout the north. Islamic militants have taken over large pieces of land in Iraq and have no intention of keeping these areas of food supply open for the people.

Many are lamenting these acts of terrorism, especially since this was a banner year for harvesting. But due to the fighting, there are many silos that sit empty because the people needed to flee for safety. Farmers have not received payment because of the conflict and this grain and wheat has not gone through processing for consumption.

So even though there is plenty of food, it is in an area not safe for most citizens and it is not ready to be properly distributed among the Iraqi people.

This conflict is believed to be an act of terrorism in the mid-east. The IS militant group has taken over the area, hoping to have a new stronghold and convert anyone who is not a Muslim over to their religion. Most Christians, even those who had lived peacefully in the area for years, fled for safety. Those who remained were forced to convert or face death.

Even those who already follow the Muslim religion are finding the conflict difficult. Women and young girls are in constant fear of being raped and beaten. Reports of gruesome procedures also abound.

The idea of the IS group is to bring fear to those who may try to fight them. The people already fear they will not make it out alive. IS has taken it a step further and cut off the majority of the country from their food supplies. In the end, this will result in the people being too scared and weak from lack of food to fight against them.

This is just one of the examples of how terrorism can effectively cut off the food supply of a country. This situation is even sadder since there is plenty of food, food that was just harvested by the hard-working waiting to be put to use. While this terrorist group is in place, however, it is likely the majority of food will go to waste and people of Iraq will starve.

CHAPTER 9:

The Steps to Food Storage

Proper food storage is important to ensure your hard work doesn't go to waste. Improperly stored food, either in the wrong location, not checking expiration dates, or storing food in the wrong containers, could lead to old and moldy food. If this happens for too long, and your family could be without food
during an emergency, even if you prepared ahead of time.

Step #1: Storing Your Food Products

Pick out the right kind of containers to store your food. This is an important part of preparation. This allows you to keep the food in a safe place until you need it. Here are some storage containers you should consider when you are ready to store your food.

6 Gallon Pails

These are perfect for food storage. They are plastic so nothing can get into them such as dust, mold, water, or animals. They also come with lids that fit tightly and you can place many items inside. You may find this is the perfect container when you want to purchase large amounts of items like flour, sugar, legumes, beans, and grains to store for the emergency. You can also get a nice liner to keep the foods from deteriorating.

Unlike boxes, you won't have to worry about the bucket getting ruined. You can place perishable food items inside with their liner and seal them up for a long time, knowing the food inside is   going to be safe from all harm. Do not open up the container again until you need the items during an emergency. The more times you open the container, the more often air will get in and have a chance to ruin your food supply.

For this project, it is best to purchase new buckets. This ensures nothing toxic was ever in the buckets that could ruin your food. You should also wash the buckets out and allow them to air dry completely before placing food inside. If you do use a previously used bucket, make sure you never use ones that had mud, sheet rock, paint, or chemicals inside. Even if you worked hard to clean these out, you are contaminating your food.

Double Enamel #10

This size of can will hold about a gallon of food. This is great if you need to hold some smaller items and you can get some plastic lids for the top; this will keep the food fresh even when you need to use it. These cans are packed with nitrogen and have an absorber packet for oxygen inside. These packets are going to take all of the oxygen out of the can, preventing insects from living in the food and hatching eggs. It is also great for protecting your food and keeping it from getting old. These cans will keep your food safe for a long time to come so it is ready whenever an emergency strikes.

Poly/Metal bags

These are good to line some of the buckets you use for storage. Sometimes it is nice to have an extra layer between the world and your bucket to ensure the food is staying as fresh as possible. Get the thick and heavy bags so they don't run the risk of breaking or getting a hole in them. You can also use these bags on their own as long as you are willing to seal them properly. This can be done using a hot iron or commercial sealer; make sure to add in some oxygen packets to keep the food fresh over time.

Oxygen Packets

If you store the food improperly and allow oxygen to get inside, you will have issues with food getting rancid or insects getting into the food and being able to survive and reproduce. When you use one of these oxygen packets in your food, you will effectively keep all the oxygen out, thereby allowing the food to last longer.

These packets look similar to a plastic tea bag, and they are the most effective way to keep your food from going bad. You need to use these within 15 minutes of opening the food and exposing it to air for the packets to work. Or you can throw these in before storing the food to ensure no oxygen is being left in to ruin the food.

Nitrogen and CO_2 Flush

If you have a welding shop near you, go and see if they will let you rent out some nitrogen gas and a CO_2 tank. For this process, flush out the food using the gas, taking extra precautions to get your hose way down to the bottom of your chosen container after you place the food in, to keep the food safe. Be careful to not get this sprayed all over.

Freezing grain

If you are worried about having insects, bugs, and other things get into your grain, you may want to consider freezing the grain to keep it safe. For most people, just leaving the grain out in the garage for a few days in the winter will get it cold enough to freeze and kill off any bugs that might try to get inside.

All of these methods are great for emergency preparation to ensure your food stays fresh and safe. You never know how long it is going to be before the emergency occurs, but you want to make sure you are getting everything ready with plenty of time to spare.

But, if you get the food early, you also need to make sure it is going to stay fresh in your storage area without getting old or having bugs and dust inside. These methods will keep the food fresh for a long time so you are ready whenever the emergency shows up.

Step #2: Rotating Food Storage to Keep Foods Safe

When you store food for an emergency, it is important to remember the food can become old and rotten if you don't take proper care of it. You cannot just throw the food down in a box in a basement where it gets wet all of the time and assume the food will still be fresh enough to eat in a couple of years. While using the containers and methods discussed above can help, it is still important to have an idea of some of the things that can make food go bad.

Some of the most common situations where food can go bad before you use it up include:

Shelf Life

When picking out food to keep in your storage, make sure to check the label. Most canned foods are going to be good for a number of years and if you process your own food correctly, you will find this food will be fine for a long time as well.

Always check the date, though. It is not going to do you any good picking selecting bulk purchases of an item that has an expiration date within the next few months. In most cases, this food is going to expire and get bad before you are able to use it during an emergency. It doesn't matter how great the bargain you got on the food; if the food is old and bad, you cannot use it.

Pick expiration dates that are at least a few years out. This gives you plenty of time if the emergency happens far into the future, and it allows you to rotate it out before it gets bad. If you store the food properly, you should be fine keeping it stored for longer, but it is still good to stick with the expiration dates to stay safe. Keep in mind the canned meats we manufacture at www.survivalcavefood.com have many years of shelf life and are the best alternatives of you want to have a great quality meat on hand.

Oxygen

Oxygen is the number one reason why your food is going to lose much of its nutritive value. No matter how healthy or sanitary your food may be, it is going to contain some enzymes that will begin to break down the food's nutritional value as soon as it is exposed to air and then its nutritional value starts to decrease.

This makes it really important for you to remove all of the oxygen around the food before you store it. Using buckets with solid lids can work well. Some people like to do vacuum seals to get rid of all the oxygen. There are a number of methods you can use, but ensuring that the food stays sealed might be the best way to ensure that the food does not begin to lose any of its important nutrients.

Bacteria

When bacteria, as well as molds and yeasts, get into your food, they can ruin your food. Bacteria is the most likely cause of your food spoiling, so you need to make sure all food is handled in the proper way to kill off all bacteria.

Luckily, there are a number of methods you can use in order to help keep the food safe including freezing, drying, dehydrating, canning, and processing. Keep in mind that when you open up the container, you need to cook and use up the food as soon as possible. Once you take the food out of its preservation method, such as out of its jar when the food was canned, the food is able to spoil quickly. If you have any foods packed in liquids, make sure to place them into the fridge right away to avoid spoilage.

Insects

In most cases, insects get into the food before it is packaged up and sealed. In other cases, you will see that insects get into the food because the package was not sealed properly. There are some insects more commonly found inside food including weevils, beetles, silver fish, moths, earwigs, roaches, and ants. These insects are able to eat the food, lay eggs inside of it, and get rid of their waste. As soon as the insects get inside and begin reproducing, you will have an infestation and the food will be inedible.

Light

When picking out containers to hold your food, pick those that have a dark color and which don't allow a lot of light get through. This means stay away from plastic buckets and glass jars. Of course, a lot of people can with glass containers; if you use these, make sure to store them in a darkened room or inside some cardboard boxes so that light is not able to harm your food.

Temperature

When you pick out a storage place, make sure to pick out one that is dry, dark and cool. This is the best for food to be stored without the food getting bad. You should also pick out a place that is going to keep the temperature about the same all year long. For most foods, keeping the temperature below 75 degrees is best, which is why many people will choose to keep their food inside a cellar or basement.

If you need to store the food in an attic, shed, or garage where temperatures are going to fluctuate often between hot and cold, you need to reduce the amount of time your food can last. The more extreme the temperatures range, the shorter the time for storage before your food is spoiled.

Moisture and Humidity

Moisture and humidity are the most common reasons your food is going to start deteriorating before you can use it. This is easily avoided if you take the right precautions and keep the food dry and safe.

For example, pick out a place that is fairly dry and doesn't get much moisture. You should also keep the food in a sealed container that can't be permeated by water if some happens to get into the area. Using canning jars, plastic containers, and other options are much better than bags or cardboard boxes when it comes to keeping your food safe and dry.

When you pick out a safe place to store your food, make sure to keep some of these things in mind. Store your food safely in an area with very little light, that is cool and will maintain a steady temperature, and ensure the food is sealed so no insects are able to get in. If you are able to keep with these tips, you will find that your food is able to last for a long time and you have some added protection you are looking for when the emergency strikes.

Step #3 How Long Does the Food Last?

Determining how long your stored food can last is important for determining how quickly you should begin preparing and how often you should rotate the food. If stored properly, many of your staples, such as wheat and pasta, can last for many years. The fact that you can store these foods for a long period of time makes them ideal for getting your emergency preparation started right away. Here are some examples of the kinds of foods you can keep for a long time in your storage area:

- Wheat—you can store this for up to 30 years
- White rice—this can last for up to 30 years when stored properly
- Corn—30 years
- Sugar—30 years
- Dehydrated carrots—25 years
- Powdered milk—25 years
- Apple slices—30 years
- Potato flakes—30 ears
- Pasta—30 years
- Rolled oats—30 years
- Pinto beans—30 years

Keep in mind you must have the perfect conditions. If you have to leave the food in the attic or garage where the temperatures change often, you will need to reduce the longevity of storage because the food will not last as long. Store the food in the right conditions, and you will find your storage is safe for a long time to come. All of the dehydrated and freeze dried meals we sell at www.survivalcavefood.com are designed to last up to 25 years if stored under optimal conditions.

Step #4: How Much Food Do I Need?

Another question many families ask is how much food they need. Most families are not used to the amount of items they are going to need in order to survive a whole year during an emergency. Yes, they may shop for their own food, but when you purchase the food a few weeks at a time, it is completely different than being prepared for a whole year at a time.

When it comes to an emergency, it is best to be prepared for at least a year. It is going to take at least this long to get food back in the grocery stores, if not longer. Depending on the severity of the issue and whether local farmers can get together to help others in some way. Actually, it might take longer.

So, let's look at the number of the items you will need to survive through an entire year of food shortage. We will assume that you need to survive for a year before food gets back into the stores. The numbers we will use are for a family of 4; two parents and two children under the age of six. If your family has more children or children who are older than 6, you will need to plan for more food than is listed here. For this imaginary family, you would need at least the following amounts of each food.

Grains:

First, let's start out with the grains. The typical family of this size will need about 450 pounds of wheat and 75 of flour to make the items they need for a year. Other things you may need include 75 pounds of pasta, 150 pounds of rice, and 75 pounds of oats.

Oils and Fats

Having some oils and fats around can be great in an emergency. You do need to have some fat to keep your body healthy and to get the nutrients that your body needs. And since you won't be eating out at fast food restaurants any longer, these fats are not going to be as hard on you.

Some of the fats you need include 12 pounds of shortening, 6 gallons of vegetable oil, 12 pounds of peanut butter, 4 quarts of salad dressing, and 6 quarts of mayonnaise.

Sugars

Sugars can be a great way to add to your cooking, and when used in moderation, and without the pastries and other goodies from the store, you will find you are still consuming a lot less than you would normally.

Some of the sugars you may want to consider for a family of this size include 4 pounds of flavored gelatin, 18 pounds of powdered fruit drink, 8 pounds of jams, 120 pounds of sugar, and 8 pounds of honey.

Milk

Milk is really important for helping keep your bones strong and are used in some of the meals you will make. Some of the milk amounts you should bring include 36 cans of evaporated milk and 180 pounds of powdered, dry milk.

Legumes

There are a lot of legumes you can place in your storage area. They are easy to store since you can store them dry and they can add a lot of protein and other nutrients to the body. Some of the things that you should bring include 12 pounds of dry soup mix, 12 pounds of lentils, 12 pounds of split peas, and 90 pounds of various dry beans.

Cooking essentials

These cooking essentials are some of the other spices you will find useful when you are trying to create a lot of great meals during the emergency. Some of these include 2 gallons of vinegar, 16 pounds of salt, 2 pounds of yeast, 4 pounds of baking soda, and 4 pounds of baking powder.

Water

When you are busy preparing for your food storage, don't forget to store up plenty of water. There is a chance you may lose some of your water privileges during the emergency, so it is best to keep some stored. For this, you should keep about 1500 gallons of water on hand plus more to rehydrate any freeze dried and dehydrated meal you have. You should also consider keeping about 4 gallons of bleach on hand. This will allow you to clean out dishes and other things to keep safe.

Things to keep in mind

At first, these might seem like really high numbers, but you can keep a few things in mind. First, it is possible to grow some of these items on your own. If you are growing a garden, the vegetables and legume storage is not as important. Some people choose to make the meals themselves rather than trying to create them when the emergency occurs. If you choose to do this, you won't need to keep as many of the staples around.

In addition, if your family isn't able to have some of the items on the list, such as peanut butter because of allergies, don't worry about adding them into your storage. This list needs to be customized to what your family will use the most. This is just meant to show you the amount of food it will take to get through a year with a family of 4.

If you feel the emergency is going to last for more than a year, you will need to keep even more staples in your possession to stay safe. The more you have on hand, even if the situation gets solved much sooner than expected, the safer you are and the more likely your family will be able to survive.

We provide a FREE FOOD CALCULATOR at www.survival cavefood.com where you can enter in the number of adults and children and it will suggest what foods and how much you need to store.

Best Alternatives to Ingredient Storage

Some of the best alternatives to storing these individual ingredients are the prepared meals we sell at www.survivalcavefood.com. These meals are ready to eat after adding water and heating them up for the suggested period of time.

Step #5: Common Mistakes of Food Storage

There are many mistakes people will make when it comes to storing their food. When you make mistakes with the food, you end up stuck when the emergency hits and none of your food is edible. Some of the most common mistakes you may be making with your emergency food storage include:

- Improper containers for storage—make sure the storage containers are going to be able to handle the food and keep all bad things out of the food. Picking sturdy containers will keep out moisture and oxygen so the food stays safe.

- Bad storage location—many people will get the food they need, and then they will keep the food in the wrong place. They will choose to go with the garage and not think about how the constant temperature changes will affect the food. They may leave the food out in the open where water and other contaminants can get in. Remember; keep the food in a cool and dry place, away from moisture and oxygen and with temperatures that keep about the same all year long to keep the food safe.

- Variety—you should get as much variety into your storage food as possible. This can make the food taste a bit better over the whole year rather than being stuck with one or two types of foods the whole time. You can even add in some vegetables and fruits to get the nutrients and a treat during that long time. This is why we suggest the prepared meals at www.survivalcavefood.com because they offer the variety you will need and it takes out the planning process since we have already done this for you.

- Missing out on water and a filtering system—you should keep at least enough water for 2 weeks in your storage area. It is best to keep even more on hand because you never know how long the emergency will last. If you assume you won't need water, you are going to get really thirsty waiting for the rain to come again. You should also have a filtering system for water in case you are worried that your water may be contaminated or you need to get it from other sources.

- Rotation—you need to make sure you rotate your food storage. You cannot go and purchase some food and assume that it is going to last forever and still be good. Take the time on occasion to look at the storage food and find out if it is good or if the expiration date is about to pass. If the food is about to get old, take it out of the storage and use it on a normal day. Make sure to add in some replacements whenever you take some food from storage.

- Forgetting equipment—make sure that you are going to have all of the cooking items that are needed to cook the food and make it during the emergency. Consider purchasing an alternative method to cook up the food. During the emergency, you may find that it is difficult to use your stove, oven, or microwave for a bit of time.

Try to be on the lookout for anything that might go wrong with your preparations before things get bad. It is much easier to fix the mistakes before the emergency rather than waiting until you are no longer able to do anything.

CHAPTER 10:

DIY Home Food Storage

Preparing for an emergency is one of the most important steps you can take to be ready when something unexpected occurs. It is important to get started as soon as possible, when it comes to storing your food, and not wait until crisis hits. Waiting around puts you in the middle of the chaos and often leaves you with nothing.

Deciding to prepare, before the emergency, is a better tactic. It allows you to get everything you need while the stores are still nicely stocked. Then, you still have time to go back and get the things you may have forgotten. You don't have to worry about   the crazy crowds, in the store, trying to take everything they can reach. You even have time to get meals prepared, or to grow   your own garden, to keep your family fed and happy.

Why Should I Prepare Ahead of Time?

No shortage of items

Waiting until everyone else is at the store, trying to get items, during the emergency is never a good idea. There are going to   be thousands of people, rushing to a store, in the hopes of finding   everything   they need. Unfortunately, most of these people are going to be stuck with just a few items if they are lucky. Despite so many people rushing to the store, there will be only a few items available to sell and no new items will come in for a while.

When you choose to get your items ahead of time, you no longer have to deal with this problem. Going out on a normal weekday, and grabbing a few items here and there as you are doing your grocery shopping, can be much easier. No one else is fighting in line to get something. In most cases, the item is going to be right where you need it to be. Of course sometimes stores run out of things you will need, but when you prepare ahead of time you can return and pick it up later and still have plenty of time.

When the emergency does occur, and everyone else is panicking, you can sit back at home where it is safe, and know that you have all the items that you need.

Going back to the store

With an emergency, it is not likely you will have a second chance to get what your family needs to survive. If you can get to the store, and grab anything at all, you are doing pretty good. This means you have one shot to get in…get out, and hopefully not get injured, before you have to find a way to survive on your own.

But for those who prepare ahead of the crisis, you won't have this problem. Was the store out of an item, but will get it in a few   days? You can go back without having to worry about the crowds. Did you forget an ingredient to some of your recipes, or remember another item that might be nice to have on hand during the emergency? Just run back out to the store when you have some time. This allows you to breathe a bit easier and not feel as panicked when the crisis arrives.

Clear-headed thinking

How clear will your head be if you wait until the disaster strikes to get your supplies? At crisis time, you will feel scared, worried, and wondering how you are going to get everything you need to survive. You will be in a panic, as you hurry to the store, hoping to find some of the items you need. Once you get to the store you will find thousands, if not more people, are having the same thoughts as you. You will see all the pushing and shoving. The realization will be that this situation is bad and you will be lucky to leave the store with anything, much less the long list of items you need, will start to dawn on you.

Instead of staying rational, you are going to start jumping right in and trying to make it through the chaos. Even if you try to remain calm, all the emotions going through it cloud your head. You are not going to have any chance of getting whatever you need and you might even head home with some items that don't make much sense.

It is never a good idea to wait until the emergency is right on top of you to decide it is time to go get these lifesaving options. It is much better to go out on a normal weekday, way before the emergency, and try to find what you need, while your head is clear and the lines are short.

First, you will find you can think clearly when there is no rush. You can sit down and make a list before going to the store, without the rush following you around. You can decide which items are going to help you and which ones are just set up as pricey gimmicks by the store. It is easier to be clear-headed without the panic and the pressure, so keep this in mind when you are considering getting your food shortage storage facility ready before the disaster.

Avoid the crowds

Avoiding the crowds at a store can be a huge benefit for starting your own home food storage in preparation of food shortages. Think of the emergency situation like a Black Friday or another big sale. Everyone is rushing to get to the market, people are getting pushed around and injured, and everyone wants to get the best prices. Of course, there are only one or two of the best deals, and unless you are quick or show up early, you will not get all the discounted items you wanted.

Preparing for a food shortage emergency is similar to this once the crisis has already struck. The difference is that during Black Friday, you simply miss out on that new TV at bargain prices, during the emergency your family is going to go without food, water, and other necessities.

Going to the market, and being prepared before the emergency, can help to avoid a rush and allows you to still get what you need.

Safety

Being in a large crowd, whom are all coming to the realization they may starve and die, is not a good idea. It is likely your safety is going to be at risk. People who are generally nice and wouldn't harm a fly are going to become vicious when their lives and the lives of their children are at stake. They will fight, cause injury, and not feel a bit bad about it. And, would you even blame them?

If you get all of your survival items, before the emergency, you will find it is much safer for you and your family. You can stay at home, already stocked up with what you need, and avoid the crowds.

Security

Preparing for the emergency long before it happens can provide you with a sense of security. You know that no matter when the emergency happens, you are prepared. You can hear about it on the news and just go down into the basement, or wherever you are storing your food, and not have to worry. Wouldn't this sense of security be fantastic for you and your family?

Less reliance on the system

Once you start to realize how fragile the whole system has become, it is much easier to start planning what you should do to get free from the system. Why let the government and others decide how much food you will get and whether or not you will be able to survive? When you prepare ahead of time, you can start to get away from the system and begin to rely on yourself. That is better than relying on any large corporation or government officials to decide who gets to eat today and who will starve tomorrow.

These are just a few of the reasons why you may want to consider setting up your own emergency food storage system, for a food shortage crisis, ahead of time. Waiting until the emergency occurs certainly will leave you without many of the necessities that you need to stay safe and sound during the emergency. Those who prepare ahead of time can stay safe, live for a long time without the system, and be the ones in charge of their own destinies.

Best Places to Store Food

Even if you have limited space in your home, there are options when it comes to picking out the perfect food storage locations. There are hidden places you can use or you can create some places of your own. This section, is going to take some time to set up, so you should look for the best places in your home to store your food until the food shortage occurs.

Best Conditions

The first thing you need to consider, when looking for food storage locations in your home, is what places will be best? You don't want to pick places with a great deal of water that will cause food to mold and render it inedible. When picking out the prime location, which is something you should do before you start to collect the food, it is to look for the best possible physical condition of the chosen locations.

In most cases, you should find a cool, dry, place to store your food. You don't want the food to be near a lot of sunlight. Consider this, you don't want a lot of people knowing you have all this stored food. Take the time to go through your home and find the place that is the coolest. This usually will be somewhere in the basement. Make sure to keep your food away from any heat source or the furnace room. The room should also not have water heaters, furnaces, refrigerators, or freezers nearby, because these are going to give off heat and increase the room temperature.

The room must stay dry at all times. If the room gets wet or damp, having the potential for moisture, the food will get moldy fast and you will end up with food that is disgusting and not usable at all. A nice properly sealed cellar, or storage space under the stairs, and even under the bed can work for you. You may also want to keep the food as close to the kitchen as possible. This makes it easy to get to, and will help you to remember to check the food and rotate it occasionally.

Basement

For those who have a home with a basement, this is a great place to store food. Most basements have at some space that's never used. Often people use the basement simply for storage, making it the perfect place; just clear out other storage and keep your food stored there without the food ever being in your way. Even if you use the basement for some living space, you may still have some storage space there or in another, out of the way corner, which is perfect for storage of food for times of crisis.

The basement is nice because the temperatures are perfect for keeping your food fresh and ready for the emergency. Again, you must ensure that the food is nowhere near the furnace, or dryer vents, since these exude moisture increasing food temperatures and can cause rust to your stored foods. A nice dark corner, which maintains a constant temperature, will keep your food safer for longer periods of time.

Also, make sure that your basement always stays dry. Basements sometimes get wet, or get really damp. Again, that harms the food you are storing. If you use the basement as a living area, you probably know whether the basement gets damp or not during the rainy season. If you don't use the basement as a living area, go down and test for dampness. You should clean, and organized the basement and seal up any leaks you discover to prepare it to be a food storage facility.

Under the Stairs

Do you really use the space under your stairs for anything important? Those who do use this space often use it for storage of unimportant things, like the Christmas decorations, or other things they forget about all together. Why not put this space, if you have it, to good use? Clear out the space under stairs of anything you don't really need and see if you can put those unimportant things somewhere else. This is the perfect time to begin your de-cluttering project you have been toying with for awhile.

You may want to consider installing some shelving to help keep your stored food off the floor and even organized. You will be surprised how many things fit under the stairs. While it might seem like a small area, many things can fit there including canned goods, camping equipment, medical supplies, and so much more.

Consider installing some hooks to hold backpacks and storage bags that should be kept off the floor.

Garage

The next place to consider for food storage is your garage. You do need to be careful about choosing the garage though. If you live in a place where it gets really hot in the summer and then cold in the winter, do not store any food in the garage. While it might stay nice and cool in the winter, it is going to get too hot in the summer, and your food will spoil when the temperatures go up.

Unless you are able to keep your garage at a consistent temperature all year-round, this is probably not the best place to store any food. But, it is a great place to store other emergency supplies that you would need during a short-term emergency. Keep things like extra paper towels, toilet paper, and even some of the seeds that you plan to use in the future for growing your own food in your garage. That will work well for you.

Attic

The attic is tricky and risky. Most attics are going to get really warm when the summer comes along. This is going to cause your food to rot. But, you can check out the attic and see if it has any potential to work out for you. Leave a thermometer in the attic and check on it a few times during the day for about a week. If the attic is insulated, and the temperature stays about the same throughout the whole day, this is a great place to store food. The attic is rarely used and no one is going to suspect you are keeping food way up there. You can store many things in this attic without having to use a lot of space in the rest of your house.

Utility Room

If you have a utility room, and it is big enough for food storage, why not use it for storing your emergency food supply. You can install some shelving above your washer and dryer to store some of the extra food you will need during an emergency. Food can go here, or you can place other items like bleach, cleaning supplies, etc. You can even leave some equipment there, that will make it easier for you to handle food shortages. Things like as roasting pans, wheat grinder, canning equipment, and a juicer could fit nicely.

If you are limited on space in your utility room, you can install shelves to hold onto blankets to keep you warm, or set up a shelf to hold onto your spices. Make this space your own, but figure out a way that will help you to use it as effectively as possible.

Closets

Turn a closet into a pantry. Of course, if you have a pantry, use it to hold the emergency food supply as well. But, if you don't have a pantry, consider organizing a closet into a new pantry.

You can choose whichever closet is the most convenient for you. For example, if you have more than one child, clear out a closet in one room and have your children share their closets. This leftover closet can start to store the food you gather and prepare for a food shortage. If you feel you are low closet space, now may be a good time to study how to eliminate clutter and learn how to clean out your home to make extra room. In most cases, you can find a way to give up a closet to store the food your family needs.

You don't want to just leave the cans of food, canned food in jars, or food in boxes on the floor, and you don't want to start to build towers of stored food. This can cause a lot of issues, especially when a tower of food topples, whenever you search for specific stored food later on. It can damage food you have on hand for the emergency. Install shelves, again I mention this, and try to organize your storage areas.

Kitchen storage

Often families choose to use their kitchens to store food that they prepare for the emergency. This is usually not the best place to store your emergency supply of food. You need to keep the food you use daily in the kitchen, not emergency food supplies; and, if you fill the kitchen with the emergency food, it becomes difficult for you to fit in your daily food sources.

Eating your stored emergency food before the emergency occurs can result in your crisis food storage being depleted too early. It is much better to find another place in the house to hold all of your food supplies for the food shortage.

If you need to use your kitchen because you are limited on storage space, try to put the emergency storage food out of the way. Use the pantry, if you can, or stick the food in a cupboard that elevated, or which you don't use very often. Remember, if the emergency food is getting in the way of your daily food, you are going to get frustrated and just give up on the whole endeavor.

When you use this strategy to put stored food in a secure place, it gets easier to store the food way up high in a cupboard or on shelves, even in the kitchen.

Make Shelves

If you are really limited on space, consider making a food shelf using food you have on hand. Get a few wooden boards with a corner somewhere out of the way can be constructed into shelves. Use food cans to be the arms of the shelf and have them support the wooden boards. Place more food on top of the boards since this is your shelving. This makes the food become a part of the furniture, giving it multiple use, rather than having food just sit around the house.

Be careful when doing this. You don't want to put too much food on the shelving as this can cause damage to the food below the shelf. When you do this sparingly it can give you some wonderful results for storing food in really limited spaces.

Under your bed

For those who really are limited on space, you need to get a bit more creative to find the right places to store food to be hidden out of the way. One place that you can choose is under your bed. Think about it; what else are you using this space for? First, sweep out the dust bunnies, then you can just slide the food to be stored right under your bed as you buy it or find some nice plastic containers to put the food and keep it a bit more organized.

Canned goods will fit well, under the bed, without taking up a great deal of space or getting in the way.

If you want to store some bigger food items under the bed, or want to rely on some bigger boxes to hold the food, raise up the frame of the bed with some concrete blocks to make additional room. Some people choose to just place their mattress on top of all the food and cover it all up before going to bed. If you choose this last option, make sure the stored food is in boxes of even height, so that you don't hurt your back in the process.

End tables

While your regular end tables are probably not going to be big enough to hold much food, you can turn some of your storage containers into end tables. If you are storing some big buckets of food, why not decorate them a bit and make them work as end tables? This can add some nice decorations to your home without taking up too much space for the food storage.

Bathroom vanity

Many bathrooms have a vanity with some storage space underneath. And in most cases, you probably aren't using much, if any, of this space. Instead of just leaving it empty; use it to store some of the food that you would like to save for an emergency. A lot of cans and other items can fit in this area and, since you aren't using it, you won't have to worry about the food getting in the way.

Before placing food in the bathroom vanity though, check the sink to ensure there is no leaks from the pipes. Check for any wet spots after running the water for a few minutes. You can also check to see if there is any moisture around the pipes. This moisture can cause rust, or other safety hazards to your food, and is not healthy. Get the faucets all fixed and the area completely dried out before you begin to store food here. The bathroom vanity is perhaps best for canned food to avoid odors from entering other food, non-canned, or food products.

Wherever you store

The place you choose to store your food is likely to vary depending on the type of home you are in and how much space you have. Some people may have extra closets or space that they don't use, which would be perfect to store some of this food in. Others may find that they have to get more creative when searching for the right place to store their food. Just get creative and use the space that you have, no matter how small. Remember that the space needs to keep a consistent temperature, preferably a little cooler, and dry. It's vital that stored foods are not going to get wet.

Many people prefer to select a place that is out of the way, as well, because this lets them go about their day-to-day business without tripping over the food. Keep some of these things in mind, and you will be set when it comes to food storage.

CHAPTER 11:

7 Simple Ways to Prepare Emergency Food Storage at Home

Preparing for a food shortage takes time, dedication, and smart thinking. Just going to the store and grabbing a few items is never enough. You need to be smart about the foods you choose for survival and how you store them to get the most out of your efforts. This chapter will look at some of the simple steps to help you prepare, for emergency food storage in your own home, for those who are not sure how to get started.

Tip #1: Foods That Pack the Biggest Nutritional Punch

When selecting foods for storage, it is best to pick those with the highest nutritional value. Your food storage area will be limited and you will want to get the most out of this space. When you pick foods with highest nutritional values, you can reduce some of the extras and still be fine. Those with high caloric content can keep you full for longer, allowing the food to last longer even when you have less stored. Some foods with high caloric and nutritional content that should be in your emergency storage include:

Nuts and seeds

These are essential for adding lots of nutrients in your diet. Try to come up with different kinds of nuts and seeds since each has different nutrients within them. When storing the nuts and seeds, keep in mind these need to be frozen, bottled, or canned to last more than a couple of months.

The amount of nutrients found in seeds and nuts is astounding and they should be included, at least occasionally, in your survival diet. These contain healthy fatty acids, Omega 3s, selenium, copper, potassium, phosphorus, magnesium, and many vitamins. These nutrients will help to maintain all aspects of your health during an emergency.

If you are looking for nuts that have a lot of calories, make sure to go with macadamia nuts and pilinuts as these have over 700 calories in 100 grams. But if you are not a fan of these, most seeds and nuts will give you the calories and the nutrients that you need.

Peanut butter

Peanut butter is a great survival food choice to have in your pantry. It contains healthy fats and quickly adds to your calorie intake without using up more than a few tablespoons of the product. Be careful with the brand you pick though. Some brands will contain a lot of sugars, additives, and even unhealthy fats. These are things to avoid during your limited survival diet. Go for the more natural peanut butters with more of the good nutrients in it to keep you healthy and not just pushing yourself to eat saturated fats.

Freeze-dried meats and Canned Meats

Meat should be a large part of your food shortage pantry and consumed daily. It is not likely you will be able to find fresh meat once the stores start to close. The stores will run out quickly, and any local farmer with cows and other livestock to sell will raise the prices significantly and still be sold out quickly as well. This will leave you without an important form of protein and nutrients.

Freeze-dried and canned meats can and should be a serious consideration when designing your food storage program. Store bought meat, even when kept in the freezer, can go bad. Canning or freeze-drying your meat can extend its life for much longer periods of time, allowing you to survive the food shortage with the proper nutrition.

You can even prepare meat at your home. Canning is a popular method that doesn't take up much time and can help you to store the meat for many years. Others may choose to dehydrate their meats. This will take a little more time, but with the proper storage, the meat will stay fresh for a long time as well.

If you are worried about properly storing your meat to keep it fresh, or aren't able to find the time, there are some companies that provide freeze-dried meats, and other food items.

Our company, www.survivalcavefood.com, has a great reputation for providing canned meats and other long-term pre-packaged foods. If you use **coupon code: book2016** you can get a substantial discount on your purchase. You can order through us, or many other companies that carry our products, and have the peace of mind knowing that your food is ready to use when a food shortage arrives.

Freeze-Dried vs. Canned Meats

At www.survivalcavefood.com you will find the finest quality canned meats available. Our canned meats are processed through a proprietary process that is much different from grocery store meats. Our meats have many years of shelf life. We do not manufacture freeze-dried meats because the quality and flavor is not up to our standards.

Freeze-dried meats are readily available in the market but are prepared to a reduced quality and taste than our canned meats at www.survivalcavefood.com

Flour

Always keep plenty of flour on hand for the emergency food shortage. Keeping bread, pastas, and other flour products on hand can take up a lot of space and some of these will go bad long before you are able to use them. With flour, you can store just one item and then make all the others that are needed.

For storage, white or whole grain flour is best. Remember, that for when you are short on space for storage and you don't have the room to store twenty different kinds of flours. Most recipes can be modified to use just one kind of flour. So, don't worry if a recipe calls for a different type of flour.

You must take extra precautions to store your flour. It is easy for dust, bugs, and other contaminants to get into your flour. Package it in small amounts and seal the flour up well so no quantity is left exposed to the elements, or to the house environment, for long. Before using the flour, go through each packet to check for dust, bugs, and other foreign items that might have gotten inside the flour.

Brown Rice

Brown rice can be used as an add-on nutrient to most of your meals. Rice if very filling and contains the nutrients and calories that your body needs without taking up a lot of storage space. Brown rice is better than white rice, because it packs in more nutrients and calories, making it possible to use less and still feel full during the food shortage.

You can add brown rice to most meals, making it very versatile. Cooking requires just water, so it is not only easy to store, but also to prepare.

Oats

Oats will also work well for your food storage. They are high in many complex nutrients meaning you will feel full on relatively few oats.

There are many ways that you can use oats with your meals. Whether you are making cookies for dessert during a food shortage, or need a healthy staple for your breakfast, oats are perfect. Oatmeal can be the perfect way to warm up for a cold day, or to bulk up if you want to save food for the long   haul.

Dried Potatoes

The Irish subsisted on a diet mainly of potatoes. Potatoes have a ton of nutrients, and one potato is often enough to keep you full   for a long time.

It is usually not a good idea to try and keep fresh potatoes on hand. Dried potatoes allow you to store large amounts without the worry of them going bad. Just add some water and you have a healthy and filling addition to any meal.

Packaged Meals

Packaged meals are perfect for food storage. There are many choices available for freeze-dried and dehydrated meals in the market. We offer a variety of gourmet (just add water) meals at our site at survivalcavefood.com. You will find that our meals are much lower in sodium than most sold in the supermarket brands, because of the high quality packaging we use to preserve our foods.

You can also choose to purchase the premade meals at the supermarket, or make some on your own. The ones at the market offer lots of options, but many contain a great deal of salt, and   can be a little unhealthy. Making the meals at home offers you any options that you like, and they can be healthier, as well as, created to handle any allergies your family may have.

Tip #2: Store in a Dry Place

When storing your food, make sure to store all food, no matter how it is preserved, in an area that is always dry. Food can easily get wet if your storage area has leaks or high humidity. There are a lot of places where you can store your food, but make sure your area is 100%

moisture-free. If you choose a basement, ensure the area hasn't leaked recently.

Take the extra precaution, and seal all windows and cracks where water may get in. Keep food away from windows, in case one of the windows gets left open during the rain. You should also avoid all areas with humidity. This includes bathrooms and laundry rooms, as moisture can seep into your foods and make them go bad before you can eat them.

Even if the storage area seems dry, ensure proper sealing and storage of all food. Some areas may have an increase in moisture or water without any notice. When you seal your food properly, moisture cannot get inside and the food will stay safe.

Tip #3: Pick Items that have long shelf lives

You never know how long before the emergency occurs. This emergency can occur tomorrow, or it can be many years before you need to dig into your food supply. You don't want the food shortage to occur and then find discover that all your stored food has gone bad and is inedible.

When picking out foods, pick out those that will last a long time. Selecting eggs, fresh fruits and vegetables, and flimsy boxed items, which are close to their expiration dates, will just result in headaches.

If you are purchasing foods from a local store for storage, check the expiration date before making the purchase. Get an expiration date as far in the future as possible. This will ensure your food will last for some time. Using this method will require some work on your part. You will need to go through your food supply from time to time and make sure nothing has expired. Simply check the expiration dates on the packages.

Sometimes making the food on your own can give you a longer shelf-life. You can use pickling, canning, freezing, and dehydrating to keep the food safe for a longer period of time.

No matter which method you use, use caution. If you ever question whether a food is good or not, get rid of it. You don't want to put your health at risk, during a food shortage, because you ate a food that was questionable.

Tip #4: Freeze-Dried Foods Work Well

Freeze-dried foods are another great way you can prepare your food to last for a long time. Whether you want to take the food backpacking or store it until the food shortage, freeze-drying is   the best option. If you do this process correctly, food that would normally last just a few weeks in a fridge can last for years in a normal storage situation. There are a number of stores that sell freeze-dried foods, including those at SurvivalCaveFood.com. Or you can choose to make some of your own freeze-dried foods at home.

If you choose to make freeze-dried foods at home, the steps are simple. You can do this process on almost any food you choose including meat, poultry, seafood, dairy, vegetables, and fruits. To freeze-dry foods, follow these steps:

1. Cut up your food into small pieces. While you don't need to make these really tiny, the large pieces are going to make the freeze dry process take longer.

2. Take out a baking sheet and lay out your food on one layer. Try to keep the pieces from touching each other to expedite the process.

3. Lay the baking sheet down flat in your freezer, turning the freezer down to the lowest possible setting. Keep the cut pieces inside the freezer for at least one week and don't open up the freezer door, if possible, for that week. The food needs to remain flat, so if you want to freeze dry   large amounts of food, you may need to consider purchasing a separate freezer to help with this process.

4. After the week is over, take the food out of the freezer and give it time to thaw. If your food has a black appearance as it

thaws, put it back into the freezer for a few more days. When the food thaws and is not dark in color, it is ready for the next step.

5. Take this food and put it into some poly-metal bags. Vacuum seal the bags and insert oxygen absorbers in all of the bags to insure freshness.

6. Label the bags with the food contents inside and the date that the food was packaged. Store at a low temperature, not allowing the food to reach above 60 degrees Fahrenheit.

Food stored with this method will last for many years as long as you maintain the proper temperatures and don't open the bag. This process is simple, and while the food does need to sit in the freezer for long, it does not take much effort on your part.

Tip #5: Remember the Water

When you prepare your food storage for shortages, make sure to store plenty of pure water. When the food shortage occurs, there is the possibility that collecting pure water will be an issue. You should collect as much water as possible to last throughout the food shortage period.

Remember that for each person in your family, you will need a minimum of 1 gallon of water, each day for hydration, plus even more for hygiene. While some family members may drink less than this, it is best to aim for at least this amount of water for a whole year if possible. If the food shortage ends before this time frame, you were simply prepared for a worst case scenario. But, you don't want to be short on water and have nowhere to get more from.

Keep your water in the proper storage containers to keep it safe. You can choose bottled water to ensure that the water is never opened until you need to use it. Bottled water has at least a few years before expiring and if you leave it closed, it can last for a considerable time past the expiration date printed on the bottle.

Another option, that can save you some money, is to use old water containers or milk jugs. Make sure to wash them thoroughly with soap and water, and then rinse them multiple times so they are ultra-clean. Then, run the water through your chosen purification system and store the water in the containers after you seal them tightly. This water comes from your own faucet so you aren't spending any extra money besides a few dollars for any storage containers purchased.

Place the date you filled the water containers on all containers, so you know how long the water has been stored before drinking it. Seal the containers tightly to keep out any dust or other particles while the water is stored.

While you are preparing your water storage, consider your water purifier. It's vital to purify any water that you plan on storing, and can be a lifesaver in case your water becomes contaminated, or you didn't store enough. During the food shortage, you should never trust any of the water that you didn't store ahead of time, even if it comes through your water faucet. This water could have germs, dirt, and other bacteria in it that can make you sick. Purified rain water also works for this. It is always best to use your purifier to keep your drinking water safe.

Tip #6: Pick Items Easy to Make and Very Portable.

When selecting your emergency food to be stored, you need to be realistic about what you can store. Picking meals that are complicated to make will just add stress to your life. Emergency storage is supposed to help you get ready for the worst, not make you want to pull your hair out.

There are a lot of great recipes you can choose for storing food for a shortage. Find a recipe that requires just a few ingredients and can be completed by adding water when the food shortage occurs. If you want to make things easier, find a store that sells emergency food supplies. You can order supplies from suppliers and not worry about making the recipes on your own.

Basically, when it comes to your emergency food storage, you should make this process as easy as possible. Easy food creation can save you time, while building up your food storage, for when the emergency occurs.

During some emergencies, you may need to leave your home. Civil unrest can make the area unsafe or a natural disaster will force you to leave your home. If you stored heavy foods that can't get wet or move easily, you may have to leave your food supply behind. The more portable your food supply is, the easier it is to carry the food with you. To make your food more portable, you can:

- Store in small amounts—These go into containers that can easily fit in a backpack and go out the door with you.

- Store the most important food near exits—Water, meals that are easy to make, and even dried meat can last you for a few weeks on the run. Keep these near an exit for a quick grab on your way out.

- Store food properly—Seal the food properly, and keep in small, safe packages. Leaving flour or sugar in their original packages results in damage if they get wet. Moving things to freezer bags can keep them safe for when you need to leave.

- Prepare a backpack with emergency food early on—When setting up your food storage, create a survival pack for each person. You may not need this, but having some survival foods and items prepared ahead of time can expedite the process if you need to leave in a hurry. Pack up enough items to get you through for a few days until you can get somewhere safe to regroup.

When your food is easy to make and portable, you can prepare   for any emergency that comes your way knowing that you can stay safe and well-fed through it all.

CHAPTER 12:

Easy Recipes to Make Your Own Emergency Food at Home

It is important to be prepared for anything, no matter what might happen. The urgency for survival mode might occur at any time. One of the best ways to be prepared is to create some of your own recipes to keep at home. You can make them at any time and keep them stored at home. When disaster strikes, you will have lots of great meals that can keep you safe and happy, regardless of all the craziness that is going on around you.

These recipes are meant to be simple to make and store. Most will require you to place the dry ingredients into a plastic bag and then pour water on them for cooking. This saves time and worry when an emergency comes. When choosing your canned meats for the recipes, check out SurvivalCaveFood.com.

Mexican Soup

Ingredients:

      1 lb. Survival Cave canned chicken

      1 ½ c. carrots, sliced
      2 c. celery, sliced
      3 cans Ro-Tel Tomatoes
      2 cans beans, kidney
      1 tsp. cumin
      3 c. corn
      6 c. water
      3 c. chopped tomatoes
      3 bouillon cubes
      3 minced garlic cloves
      1 Tbsp. canning salt

Directions:

1. Place all of the ingredients inside a large pot and bring it to a boil. Reduce the heat and let it simmer for about 15 minutes.

2. While these ingredients are cooking, wash and sterilize 7 canning jars with hot water.

3. When the soup is ready, ladle it into the jars, leaving about an inch on the top. Place the lids on top and then wash off the jars to keep them clean.

4. Use either a pot with boiling water or a pressure canner to seal up the jars. Take them out of the heat and wait to hear the lids pop close before storing for later.

Chicken and Vegetable Soup

Ingredients:

> 1 tsp. black pepper
> 3 tsp. salt
> 1 c. carrots, sliced
> 3 qt chicken broth
> 2 diced celery ribs
> 1 diced onion
> 2 Tbsp. oil
> 14 oz. Survival Cave canned chicken

Directions:

1. Inside of a large pot, heat up some oil and cook the celery and onion to make tender. And the rest of the ingredients along with the chicken and cook until heated thoroughly.

2. Ladle this soup into some jars, leaving a bit of space and secure the lids. Process the cans for about 75 minutes in a pressure canner with 10 pounds of pressure. Store somewhere safe once done.

Basic Meatballs

Ingredients:

    2 qt. boiling water or broth
    2 cans (28oz.) Survival Cave canned ground beef
    28 ounces of beef broth
    ¼ tsp. pepper
    1 Tbsp. cooking oil
    1 Tbsp. salt
    1 c. chopped onion
    ½ c. water
    1 c. bread crumbs, soft
    1 egg

Directions:

1. In a sauté, pan place the oil and onions and heat until translucent

2. Take out a bowl and combine the eggs, bread crumbs, water, cooked onion, salt, and pepper together. Let this soak up the water for a few minutes.

3. Add in the beef and mix it together well. Shape this mixture into 24 meatballs. Place these into a baking pan and bake the meat for about 15-20 minutes at 425 degrees.

4. When these are done, give them some time to cool down. Pack into some prepared canning jars, leaving a bit of space. Add the broth or water to the jars before securing the lids.

5. Process the mixture for about 75 minutes in a pressure canner. Cool down before storing.

Instant Chicken Couscous

Ingredients:

   1 ½ c. water
   ¼ tsp. salt
   1/8 tsp. pepper
   ¼ tsp. garlic powder
   1 ½ tsp. poultry herb blend
   1 ½ tsp. powdered flavor base, chicken
   1 Tbsp. onions: freeze dried
   ½ c. mixed vegetables, freeze dried
   1/3 c. Survival Cave canned chicken
   1/3 c. couscous
   1/3 cup of available herbs Directions:

1. Add water to pot and bring to boil. Pour in the ingredients and let them cook for about 10 minutes or until soft.

2. Plate and sprinkle with available herbs. Serve warm.

Fiesta Chicken and Rice

Ingredients:

 1 ½ c. water
 ¼ tsp. salt
 1/8 tsp. pepper
 ¼ tsp. garlic powder
 ½ tsp. cilantro
 ¼ tsp. oregano
 ¼ tsp. cumin
 1 ½ tsp. chili powder
 1 ½ tsp. chicken flavor base
 1 Tbsp. dried onions
 ¼ tsp. minced jalapeno
 ¼ c. tomatoes: freeze dried
 ½ c. corn, freeze dried
 1/3 c. Survival Cave canned chicken
 2/3 c. brown rice

Directions:

1. Add water to pot and bring to boil.

2. Add all ingredients to boiling water and let cook for 20 minutes

3. Season with salt and pepper and serve

Creamy Alfredo

Ingredients:

- 1 ¼ c. water
- ¼ tsp. salt
- 1/8 tsp. pepper
- ¼ tsp. garlic powder
- 2 Tbsp. cornstarch
- 2 Tbsp. instant buttermilk powder
- 3 Tbsp. Parmesan cheese
- 1 ½ tsp. chicken flavor base
- ¼ c. chopped mushrooms
- ¼ c. Survival Cave canned chicken
- 1 c. broken pasta, thin

Directions:

1. Add all ingredients, except Survival cave chicken, to pot and bring to boil for 10 minutes

2. Add chicken and cook for 5 minutes more or until heated through

3. Serve and enjoy.

Curry Rice

Ingredients:

    1 ½ c. water
    ¼ tsp. salt
    1/8 tsp. pepper
    ¼ tsp. garlic powder
    1 ½ tsp. curry powder
    1 ½ tsp. chicken flavor, powdered
    1 Tbsp. onions: freeze dried
    ¼ c. mixed vegetables, freeze dried
    ¼ c. chopped cashews
    1 (28oz) can Survival Cave chicken
    2/3 c. brown rice

Directions:

1. Place all ingredients, except chicken, in pot and bring to boil for 15-20 minutes.

2. Add chicken and cook additional 5 minutes or until heated through

3. Serve and enjoy.

Thai Noodle Meal

Ingredients:

4 c. water
¼ tsp. salt
1/8 tsp. pepper
1/8 tsp. Cayenne pepper
¼ tsp. ground ginger
¼ tsp. garlic powder
1 ½ tsp. cilantro
3 Tbsp. peanut butter, powdered
1 ½ tsp. chicken flavor, powdered
¼ c. mixed vegetables, freeze dried
¼ c. roasted peanuts, chopped
¼ c. Survival Cave canned chicken
1 c. broken pasta

Directions:

1. Add water to pot and bring to boil.
2. Add broken pasta and cook until tender (about 12-14 minutes.
3. Drain pasta and reserve 1 cup of water.
4. Add remainder of ingredients and heat completely, adding reserved water as need to get a creamy consistency (about 5 minutes)
5. Put on plate and enjoy

112

CHAPTER 13:

Simple Hidden Home Gardens

One of the best things you can do, in order to make sure there is enough food to last for the complete length of the emergency, is to work on a home garden. During the emergency, you need to keep the garden hidden from public view so no one tries to take the food from you and steal all your hard work. There are a lot of steps to get the hidden home garden set up to keep you safe. This chapter is going to look at some of the things that you should work on when you are ready to start this garden.

The Benefits of a Home Garden During Disaster

Some of the benefits of creating your own home garden include:

Growing your own food

The first benefit of a home garden is you are able to grow your own food. With some careful planning, think about how much food you will be able to plant into your garden. Even if you are in a tiny apartment, there are many places where you can place your garden and watch the plants grow. You can get a lot of food growing in your garden, without relying on the stores, and you even get to pick the fruits and vegetables that you would like to use. This can give you a lot more control than you would be able to have in any other situation.

Reduce your need on stores

When you grow your own garden, you don't need to rely on the markets as much. This is great to do even before the emergency starts. For example, if you like a certain type of tomato, or are never able to find peppers in your store, you can grow them at home and never have to go without them when the store is low on produce.

This becomes even more important when you are dealing with an emergency. The stores are not always able to get food for a long time during crisis time. But with your hidden garden, you can   keep growing food, regardless of the turmoil going on all around you, and have some great options when it comes to food options.

More variety of foods

When you prepare for the food shortage, you will be more limited on the foods that you can eat. You have to find foods that can be stored for a long time and that won't go bad. You also need foods that are versatile and can be added into many different meals. And, while this is the most effective way to get prepared for the worst case scenario, it can also lead to some boring choices if you are stuck with them for a long period of time.

Luckily, when you grow your own hidden home garden, you can have a much bigger variety of vegetables and fruits to grow. You can add in other types of nutrients and ingredients that you are able to get from your own home garden. If you are tired of the staples, you can grow some tomatoes or some fruits that can add a bit more flavor to your meal meals. This can make the waiting time until stores reopen much easier for you to handle.

Fresh fruits and vegetables

Freshly grown fruits and vegetables are the best reasons to grow your own garden. These are full of the nutrients you need, plus   the taste is going to be amazing when you compare it to all the other foods you have been consuming. You can also pick out the ones you want to use from your garden to make the choices specific to your own wants and needs.

More vitamins

Consuming enough vitamins and minerals, during survival, can be a mighty challenge. You'll want to make sure you are staying healthy; but, finding foods that are high in the nutrients your body needs, without having trouble keeping them safely stored is almost impossible. While a nice multivitamin can work wonders, it is often best if you are able to get these nutrients from the fresh produce that you grow yourself.

When you grow your own garden, you will be able to enjoy some of the best nutritious foods that you can conceive of for your body. No matter what kind of produce you choose, you will see that your body is getting a lot more nutrients compared to the other foods you are eating because fresh produce is the highest in nutritional value.

Tools Needed to Start a Home Garden

Now that you have decided that it is time to get started on your indoor garden, something that you can easily start long before an emergency strikes, it is time to get all the gardening tools needed to keep your indoor farm growing strong. Some of the tools that you should consider having include:

- Trowel—This is like a shovel, but it is a smaller version that will work for the smaller pots and containers used for inside gardening. It also will store a bit easier. You can get ones that are metal or plastic to work for your garden. Use this to dig holes, scoop out soil, and even to get rid of weeds.

- Hand rake—This is a smaller version of your garden rake that can be good for leveling the soil, loosening it up, and to spread out the nutrients that are inside.

- Pruning shears—These are basically just scissors that you will be able to use in order to get rid of the dying plant parts. They are going to be sharp with a curved blade so that can make a really clean cut. You want to get rid of the dead plant parts quickly, so that they don't take up space and reduce nutrients from the healthy part of the plant that will bring you the nutrients that you need. If you are going to have an extensive garden, make sure to get pruning shears of high quality.

- Trays, containers, and pots—The kinds that you will often use depend on how you plan to set up your garden. For example, if you are using a little ledge in your house, a pot might work, while a window might work with a window planter. There are a lot of different containers that can hold your plants, so look at your space and see what will most effectively fit the in your space.

- Wire and stakes—Even though you are growing plants inside, you need to make sure that they are getting the support that they need. Some plants are still able to grow quite tall and might need a bit of wire to help them to stay straight until they are a lot stronger.

- Mist sprayers—These are often more effective when compared to using a watering bucket. You can use just a spray bottle, like that for your hair, or find one that is a bit fancier. The point is to safely water your plants without making a mess, or causing a lot of water to spill all over the place.

- Indoor lighting—Even if you are able to keep the plants by the window, and give them plenty of sunlight, you should still consider some indoor plant growth lights. The plants need a lot of light, and it is hard to give them the sunlight that they need, in order to grow strong and the use of indoor grow lights can make the process much easier. Try out a few different kinds to ensure that your plants are getting exactly what they need to thrive.

- Soil—Pick out a good planting soil. Go with one that has a lot of nutrients. You can even mix it in with some outdoor dirt to get the best results for your plants.

- Movable containers—You might consider doing this in order to move your plants around. This is great if you are low on space or you would like to move the plants outside on occasion to get some better lighting. Make sure to get some containers that are really sturdy and can handle the weight.

Get your tools ready early so that you are able to get your garden started and growing strongly before an emergency occurs. Using these recommended tools will make your garden so much easier and it can be a fun activity for the whole family.

Best Foods to Grow

Creating your garden is vital to keeping you healthy and providing variety in your meals. But, which plants should you consider to ensure that you are getting the most out of your indoor garden? Some of the fruits and vegetables you should consider for your indoor garden include:

1. Avocados—These have a lot of the nutrients that your body needs including vitamin A, carotenoids, vitamins B6 and E, and healthy fats. Pick a dwarf avocado plant for best results, use a little sand at the bottom of the soil, and water on a regular basis to get the best results.

2. Carrots—Carrots provide many of the nutrients that your body needs to stay healthy. You can find carotenoids, vitamins K, C, A, and B6 as well as potassium, manganese, folate, niacin, and thiamine in carrots. Carrot seeds work well for planting in a box that is tall, at least a foot in height, because carrots can grow underground.

3. Lemons—Keeping fruits in the diet is challenging. Lemons are a super food you need to pack in daily doses of antioxidants and vitamin C while also helping your home smelling amazing.

Pick plastic or clay pots with holes at the bottom and fill up with stones to give the lemon tree roots circulation. Water often, but don't overdo it; misting sprays work best for lemons. Lemon trees take time to develop, grow, and bear fruit. Be patient.

4. Salad greens—Arugula, red leaf, romaine, spinach, and iceberg lettuce all count and can provide you the iron, folate, and a ton of vitamins. Use these as a side dish to your favorite emergency meals.

5. Tomatoes—Tomatoes can work well in any meal you want to create. Place them on a sandwich, in a salad, or in a casserole and you get all the antioxidants and lycopene that your body needs.

6. Herbs—Herbs can add a lot of flavor to your meals and growing an herb garden really doesn't take up much space. Consider growing mint, basil, ginger, and rosemary as these do well inside your home, without a lot of light or space, while adding flavor to your meals.

7. Strawberries—Berries can do well growing inside and provide your body with important nutrients. These do take a bit longer to grow compared to other produce so be prepared to grow other foods too.

8. Cucumbers—Eat these on a fresh salad or you can eat them as pickles later!

9. Radishes—Radishes grow quickly, whether they are grown indoors or outdoors, and you can enjoy them in a few short weeks. They like to grow in the sun so take them outside on hot days.

10. Potatoes—Filling and delicious, you can grow your own potatoes in a garden. This helps to save on room in storage and since they're fresh, you are getting the most nutrients possible.

Choose any fruit and vegetable that you would like to grow inside your home. Having an indoor gardening plan can help make your food supply last longer while offering you more variety and nutrients to your meals.

Best Places to Hide Your Home Garden

The point of an indoor garden is to hide your indoor farm from noisy neighbors. During an emergency, leaving food outside in a traditional garden invites others to take advantage of you. If you were desperate for food, would a small gate stop you from getting food to your family? Growing the garden inside can prevent others from even knowing the garden exists, allowing you and your family to have plenty of extra nutritious food during a food shortage crisis.

But, where should you hide this garden? Here are some great ideas on how to hide a garden in your home and even use it as part of the décor.

Window sills

The windowsill is a great place to place your plants. They get direct sunlight and are out of the way at all times. Find a windowsill that has a nice ledge to provide support for the plants so none of them fall off.

Pick out a window that gets plenty of sunlight; the more sunlight the better. Your plants may do well indoors, but they still need as much sunlight as you can give to them. Also, ensure that you are watering the plants sufficiently if you are giving them direct sunlight. This will require a little extra water storage.

Centerpieces

Use your indoor garden as a part of your décor. Find decorative pots and planters to grow the plants before placing them around the house. Place one in the middle of the dining room table and then daydream about eating the delicious food once it has grown. Place plants on an end table, coffee table, or somewhere else that could use a little homey touch and that you aren't using often.

Corner Nooks

Corners are the most underutilized areas in the home. Often it is difficult to shove something in the corner because of size or fit. Your plants can fit into this area easily with a little planning.

My first suggestion is to find a corner nook shelf and place your pots on there. This doesn't take up much space and realistically; you weren't using the nook much in the first place. Then, have different-sized plants placed attractively around your home to make them a part of your décor.

If you can't find a nook, consider getting some plant boxes that will fit in the corner. You can make your own little shelf with plant boxes, placing them strategically in the corners to look nice.

Hanging them from the Ceiling

For those who are short on space, consider hanging the pots from the ceiling. Since you are not using this vertical space very much anyway, it can be a great way to keep the plants off the floor and out of your way. Hang them up high to avoid hitting your head and you can almost forget the plants are there. But, don't forget to water them.

Pick out a planter that can be hung from the ceiling. There are options that allow you to hang your plants outside and these work really well inside as well. Find some planters that are sturdy and won't fall down or you will end up with a mess.

Be careful when you are watering these plants though. Giving them too much water can result in a watery mess on your floor.

Wall Space

Do you have some wall space that is blank? Have you been wondering what to do with it? Do you feel at a loss? There is much that you can do with your plants that will add to the décor of your walls. Not only are you decorating, but also you are growing food that will keep your family well fed.

There are a number of options for this. Some people like to get a few small shelves and just place the pots on the shelves. You can find some colorful or unique pots that will match your current décor. You can hang the pots strategically around the walls to get a cool design. Or, you can frame other pieces of interest like a graphic with small pots around it. Have some fun with this and see how it matches the décor in your home.

Bookcases

If you have a few bookcases that are empty in your home, you can use them to place some of your interior garden that growing food plants. Make sure this is sufficiently close to your windows to catch sunlight, or bring out a few grow lights to ensure the plants are getting all of the light needed to grow food for you.

There are a lot of unique spaces where you might be able to keep more plants in your home. Get creative and use any space available in your home. Most people feel that a garden should go outside; while this would be ideal, but because of the upcoming food shortage and crisis, people will take your food and all of your hard work will be for nothing. By using the space in your home you'll see how much easier it is to prepare for emergency food shortage in a secure setting that you have total control.

Seeds

While you are planting your garden, remember to save all of the seeds. You won't be able to go out to any store to buy more seeds. But, after the first harvest is done, but you will still need to grow more food until the emergency is over. Luckily, all the fruits and vegetables you are going to grow will give you seeds. As you harvest the food, take the seeds out and preserve them. This offers you an endless cycle of food that can last years, even after the emergency is over.

CHAPTER 14:

Canning to Preserve Food

Canning is jars is perhaps the greatest method to store food for when you want to have some flexibility of diet. It improves your storage capacity, and gives you diversity in what you will during the food shortage. Canning offers fresh food, prepared and stored, from a garden that you control, from meats that you cook, and from items you've purchased at the local market. If you are growing a garden, canning in canning jars is the easy to get to and will keep your fruits and vegetables safe for a long period of time.

Many people preparing for an emergency choose to use canning to get ready. The entire key to canning, is that fresh fruits and vegetables, meats, chicken, fish, etc. can have their life extended through a process of preparation – and that process can be one that makes your food extremely tasty, instead of dry, boring, and bland

The method is as simple as this – cook your food, as if you are going to eat it, but instead, put them in canning jars (typically Mason Jars) and then seal it properly and the food will last in storage for several years and years. Mason Jars are inexpensive and this method allows people who are into preparedness and survival to grow and store more food, and they, therefore, are ready for any food emergency that might occur.

By canning your food, you will increase variety, flavors, and just how long you can survive as compared to your unprepared neighbors.

You can do canning before or during a food shortage, whether you are preparing your own homegrown fruits and veggies (and meats, etc.) or whether you have bought items at the market or from survivalcavefood.com

You'll need a large quantity of Mason Jars to get the process going. Preparing well in advance of a food crisis is a brilliant idea. Go to the store, get your Mason Jars, and cook extra food at every meal, and then can the excess and put it into storage. This is the mindset of being prepared. In this case you will be canning a little bit at a time.

If you have a feeling that you must ultimately be prepared ASAP get your food stuffs together, and do a whole weekend, or several, of cooking and canning and fill up your storage spaces with your canned goods in preparation for the upcoming Great American Food Shortage.

When you think of America being impacted by droughts and floods, it must give you pause to think that the problem of food shortages is going to be a reality and soon. The changing weather, global warming, planetary changes, all give good reasons for you to be prepared. Do not procrastinate – take action now and be ready.

This chapter will help you look at getting ready for the food shortages by discussing the basics of canning and why you must consider using it to help you to prepare for survival.

The Basics of Canning

We've already discussed the importance of creating an indoor garden to have more healthy food that you will require for your immediate needs. You want to be prepared and to have foods available for as long as the food shortage continues and a home garden is probably the most efficient way to do that.

Let's talk about canning your food. Canning is a natural and healthy process of food preservation. Done right, your canned foods will last years, actually several years, and it will still taste fantastic when you decide to eat it. I can remember going into the basement of my grandparents and finding shelves lined with Mason Jars with all kinds of fruits and vegetables, and every now and then we were treated to some canned peaches or apricots – and the taste was always purely delightful.

Why have a food shortage if you must eat food that tastes like cardboard, when you can have this outstanding alternative when you get prepared in advance?

From a preparedness point of view, you must begin canning your own food long before the food shortage becomes reality. With the harvest from your own garden you should can all the fruits and vegetables possible; also can prepared meats, sauces, and more.

Then store what you've canned in a safe place. This will ensure that the food tastes delicious and nutritious. With your food supplies in a state of readiness, you are ready whenever the emergency strikes, and you will survive. If you think about it, your food will be fantastic and almost as if there is no shortage in your own home. One thing that is important is that you tell no one that you have all this food in storage for an emergency. Keep this secret to yourself.

If there happens to be a drought, a blizzard, or a flood, and your food supplies dries up – you will be glad you have prepared. You'll be even happier that you kept your preparedness secret from everyone else. Encourage your spouse and children to keep this information secret as well.

Now, if you are going to can during the food shortage, realize you'll be under a bit more stress. You'll have to maintain your garden, move it indoors if it was outdoors, and rather quickly can all the extra food you are producing. This is not the optimum way of preparing for a food shortage, however, will work for a short- term food shortage crisis.

What you need

To start your canning process, you need a few supplies. It is best to get these supplies at the store or online before the food shortage. Most grocery stores will have these supplies, making it easier to find what you need. Purchase these well ahead of time and use them to get your food ready for the emergency that's coming. Some of the supplies that you will find helpful in this process include:

- Canning jars—The first thing needed for this project is canning jars. Mason jars are, in my opinion, the best option and are found in most local stores. There are other options, but choose ones that are produced from thick glass to prevent cracking and breaking. Use only ones that seal properly during the processing part. Otherwise, you will have spoiled food.

- Funnel—Pouring the liquefied parts of your prepared fruits and vegetables into a jar will be difficult without a funnel. Instead of making a mess, buy a sturdy funnel that you can use to pour the liquids straight into the canning jar without spills.

- Lid wand—The lid wand helps you to get prepared lids and rings out of the hot water during sanitization. The lid wand keeps your fingers safe from boiling water.

- Ladle—Ladles help when it comes to stirring your foods during the process of cooking, or to ladle the foods bigger pieces of food into your prepared canning jars. Get a ladle that is big enough to fill the jars quickly and that can work well with your funnel.

- A big pot—Canning is never complete without using a big pot to cook and seal. Many recipes will ask you to boil the fruits and vegetables that you are using in your recipes. You can also do the process of sealing the jars in a big pot if you don't have any equipment to seal them. A really large pot will hold more jars and save time.

- Clean cloths—These are useful for cleaning off the jars after you fill them up. Leaving food on the outside of the cans creates a mess and could prevent the jars from sealing properly. Wash each jar before proceeding.

- Tongs—Never reach into the hot water of your big pot using bare hands. Tongs can help you grab what you need. Use the tongs to get the jars out of the water during the processing phase.

- Pressure canner—Some people prefer to use a pressure canner for the processing stage rather than just boiling water in a big pot. This is because the pressure canner can reach higher temperatures, ensuring a proper seal to which guarantees the good stays fresh and healthy.

Steps to begin canning

Canning is basically a method to store food in its most tasty form, and done right it will provide you and your family with all the food you will need. If you have never done canning before, you will be surprised at how easy it will be. Some of the steps that you should take to properly can your meals include:

1. Sterilize Canning Jars

Even if you purchase brand new jars, make sure to sterilize them before using. Dust and dirt can easily get into the jars if they are not sterilized and sealed them properly after processed. You don't want damage to your food. No one wants to plan ahead and prepare food, just to open it during the food shortage and find out the food has been contaminated by foreign substances.

Boiling water is the best option for sterilization. Use your big pot and boil some water. Now place all the jars, lids, and rings inside. Boil these for about ten minutes before turning off the heat. Then, you can take the jars out, but leave the lids and rings in the hot water so they don't get contaminated.

If you are planning on canning right away, your jars are ready to use and you can fill them up with your favorite food immediately.

If you plan on using these jars at another time, let the jars air dry and then store them in a safe place until you are ready to use them.

2.   Prepare the food

This step will vary depending on the foods you use. In most cases, canning the foods right after the harvest and cooking is done is the best way to ensure you preserve the greatest amount of nutrients from the foods you prepare and keep the best flavor. Fruits and vegetables that aren't prepared and canned when the fruits and/or vegetables are fresh begin to lose their nutrient content quickly, making them less healthy compared to food prepared and canned right away.

Select your perfect recipe to help you properly prepare your foods. There are many options that you can use and it depends on what you plan to do with the food. For example, tomatoes are useful for canning and you can keep the tomatoes as tomatoes, or make them into pizza sauce, spaghetti sauce, ketchup, tomato soup, and so much more. A recipe book for canning will help you to find out the best way to prepare your produce for the food shortage.

3.   Fill up the jars

Once the food is cooked and ready for canning, it is time to get them into your jars. This method is simple, but make sure you follow a few important rules. First, don't fill up the jars all the way to the top. When you go through the cooking phase, your food will begin to expand during the boiling. If you fill the jar all the way to the top, your jar may burst open or not seal properly. Usually leaving about half an inch on the top will allow the food contents to expand safely without breaking or shattering your jars.

Next, check to see that no air bubbles are present in the jars when you seal them. These bubbles can result in the food not processing properly. The best way to prevent against this is to pack the food tightly into the jar.

Before sealing the jars, wipe them down. You don't want your   food stuck between the lid and the ring. When food gets stuck on the jar, it can prevent the jar from sealing correctly and your food will spoil.

4. Processing the jars

Now that you have filled up the jars and sealed them properly, it   is time to complete the canning process. To finish the process, the jars basically are placed in high temperature water in order to seal the lids and that will keep the contents in perfect condition.

A pressure cooker is best for processing the jars, but you can also do the processing in your big pot with boiling water. When using the pressure cooker, place a bit of water inside and let it heat up to about 180 degrees. Don't let the water get hotter than this at first; you can raise the temperature soon enough but the moderate heat helps the glass containers adjust. Do not let the jars touch or bang together against each other inside the pressure cooker.

Once everything is set properly within the pressure cooker, bring your water to a boil and finish the processing of the canning jars. Your particular recipe should tell you how long the jars need to be heated for before the process is complete. Do not bring the jars out early or you risk ruining the sealing process. You might hear a popping as the jars begin to seal while they are processing. Most of the sealing will occur after you take the cans out of the water, so don't feel worried if you don't hear the popping sound indicating proper sealing earlier on.

5. Remove the jars

Once your jars have heated for the correct amount of time, take them out of the pressure cooker and allow them time to cool down on a solid surface. You may want to lay down a towel or use a rack to catch any water that drips off. Be patient with this step; sometimes it can take a couple hours for the canned jars to cool down.

During the cooling down stage, some popping of the jars will occur assuring a good seal and ensuring that your food will taste great when you open the jar.

Once the jars cool down, you can test whether they are properly sealed. Just press down in the middle of the jar's lid. If it stays sturdy, the jar was properly sealed and you can store it. If a few jars did not seal all the way, place these in the fridge and eat them instead of storing them.

6. Labeling the jars

Before placing the canned food in your storage area, make sure that every jar is properly labeled. You may think you will remember what is in every jar, but after a few months or longer, you will certainly forget. It is best to label the jars the same day as you cook them. When you are sure what is in each jar, label it to avoid any unnecessary risk.

Put as much on the label as you can. This usually includes the name of the food as well as the date that you canned the food. This will make it easier to determine what is in each jar when you need to get them from storage and will help you to select the oldest food before it goes bad.

Special labels can be bought in the canning aisle that will fit perfectly on the jars. Some people will buy labels that can be erased for future use once the food is consumed. Since you are not able to reuse the lids, once the can is opened, it is sometimes easier to just put the information on the lid to save some time and money. Once every jar is labeled, take the jars to your storage area and use the FIFO method. FIFO stands for first in, first out. If this is your first canning experience, the freshly canned foods go in the front and anything you can at a later date goes in the back. This ensures that you never waste food and eat the oldest food first.

Canning is not a complicated process. As long as you read the instructions on your recipe to ensure that you cook the food long enough, you will be setup to have some delicious and nutritious food whenever there is a food shortage. And, since you can save your canned foods for a long time when done properly, you never have to worry about running out of delicious, homemade food.

Types of Foods to Can

Almost any food you can imagine can be canned and preserved for later use. For those who want to get a head start on any potential food shortages in the future canning is the best way to go. Some of the best options, in terms of ease of canning and nutritional value include:

- Tomatoes—When you first think of canning, you should think of tomatoes. Tomatoes can work exceedingly well   for survival preparation. They are easy to can and take just minutes to prepare. You will get a ton of nutrients from them, making them one of the best forms of produce to keep on hand. In addition, tomatoes can be used in many dishes including pastas, Mexican dishes, soups, pizzas, salads, and more. If you only have time for one type of produce to can, the tomato should be your #1 choice.

- Pumpkins—Pumpkins are a little trickier to can in an emergency considering they need a lot of outdoor space   to grow. But, if you are preparing for a food shortage ahead of time and have some outside space for a garden, they can be a great addition. Pumpkins have a lot of nutrients and are able to be canned really well. You can store jars of pumpkin, during the emergency, to use in soups and some favorite seasonal items; then you can enjoy the seeds as a snack.

- Cucumber—Enjoy cucumbers in a variety of ways. Some people like to just store cucumbers as an extra vegetable for their meals. Some turn them into pickles to make them last longer and for a different taste. While pickling is a   little different than canning, they use a lot of the same methods of food preservation.

- Jams—For those who have a lot of fruits on hand, jams are a great way to store them. These can work well on any desserts you may prepare, during the food shortage, or you can have them on bread during breakfast. Pretty much any fruit can be turned into a jam, so make different kinds of jam for variety. You can even find some sugar-reduced recipes to make your jams a bit healthier.

- Eggs—Getting fresh eggs during a food shortage can be really difficult unless you plan on keeping chickens around. The problem with live chickens though, unless you live out away from people, is that your neighbors may come and steal your chickens. Instead of losing out on the important protein and other nutrients from eggs, consider pickling eggs. Pickling keeps the nutrients intact, and provides you with healthy eggs to use during breakfast or in other recipes during the food shortage.

- Meats—You may can your meats to save for food shortages. While some people choose to dehydrate meats to save, sometimes canning is a better option. With dehydration, you have to be extra careful that the moisture in the air isn't very high or your meats will be ruined. When you can your meats, this is not as big challenge. You can process any type of meat that you like including beef, jerky, chicken, fish, and more.

- Peppers—Peppers of all types can go through the processing phase. These have a lot of vitamins and nutrients and you can add peppers to soups, pastas, casseroles, and salads during the food shortage.

- Corn—Fresh corn is amazing when added to healthy dishes. But, growing corn in your home, during the food shortage, can present a challenge. This is a vegetable that you should consider canning before the food shortage occurs. This permits you to keep corn on hand during the shortage.

These are just a few of the foods that you may consider when it comes to canning. There are many recipes that will allow you to can any fruit, vegetable, and even other food products that you want.

CHAPTER 15:

Commercially Prepared Food, a Great Source for Food Storage

As we have discussed throughout this entire book, it is important to prepare for the worst when it comes to a food shortage. Get started right away, even if an emergency doesn't happen for years down the road. It is the best way to ensure you have all the food you and your family needs ahead of time.

Benefits of Choosing Commercially Prepared Food

There are many benefits of choosing commercially- prepared food to expand your food storage. Just because you are short on time, or worried about your food preservation techniques, does not mean you can't be prepared for when the food shortage occurs. Some of the benefits of going with commercially- prepared food includes:

Saves time

Most people live busy and somewhat chaotic lives. Finding time to make enough food for a whole year or more when dealing with work, school, family, and other responsibilities can be virtually impossible. Getting enough food for a few days of storage is an accomplishment, and often you will be stuck without increasing the amount of your food storage necessary for a pending food shortage crisis.

Choosing commercially prepared foods can be a great option if you're just too busy to do the work yourself. You can order all the food you need, in just a few minutes online, and know your family is protected. You can continue with your regular schedule knowing that all your food storage needs are taken care of.

Reassurance

When you purchase your food for storage from a reputable company like our own company: www.survivalcavefood.com, you have the reassurance the food is prepared and packaged properly. For those who have never canned, freeze-dried, or dehydrated food, this reassurance can be a real time-saver and will set your mind at ease.

If you've never done any of these processes, you may be worried that you are not doing everything right and the food won't last long-enough to be used. When you choose a company to do this work for you, you know the food will be fine and last a long time, and be ready whenever the food shortage begins.

Low-cost

Because you can purchase your food storage items in bulk, there is often a large discount offered on your purchases. When you purchase enough products, or plan your purchases wisely, you will be able to get your food storage items for a lower price than purchasing them at your grocery store. Saving money while keeping your family protected, during a food shortage, can make the whole situation easier.

Peace of mind

When you choose commercially prepared foods, you have the peace of mind of knowing your family is protected with their food necessities. You can order the exact amount of food you will need for a year, and know it will arrive safely. Rather than worrying about getting to the store, having time to prepare food, or any other issues of food storage, everything is taken care of for you.

Pick a Company Who Cares

When it comes to the safety and security of your family during a good shortage, it is important to choose the very best. That is why many people choose SurvivalCave.com for all their commercially- prepared survival food needs. Our company offers a large range of survival meals, freeze-dried foods, and long-term storage canned meats.

All products have a shelf life of many years so you know the food will be fresh and ready to enjoy whenever you need them! At most, all you need is water to make a delicious meal for your whole family with these great products.

Being prepared for an emergency takes knowledge, time, and the perfect products to not only feed your family, but to keep all of them healthy. All of our canned meats and prepared foods are ready to eat from the moment you take them off the shelf. Our freeze-dried products are low in sodium and are very healthy, and even our fruits are available to keep on hand for fast and easy nutrition, even during a food shortage.

Our canned meats are low in sodium, low in fat, low in cholesterol and taste great.

Survival Cave foods are available nationwide, making it easy to find exactly what you are looking for, or you can purchase the food at our website at www.survivalcavefood.com.

Want to see save some money on your purchase? Use code: **book2016** to get an automatic discount just because you are reading this book.

Conclusion

There are many situations happening in our world that should leave the average person with a feeling of concern. When these situations are left on their own, it may seem like poor management, but nothing too serious that should worry any of us.

A food shortage can occur at any time if just one of these situations gets bad enough. There are too many variables with only a few people in charge on top of the problem. A natural disaster with poor governmental support can knock out a food supply pretty quickly.

The Chinese, or terrorists, could get ahold of our food supply and poison thousands in no time.

The people in charge of storing and distributing food throughout the world could get angry and create a shortage of any or all of the foods you enjoy each day.

I am not a fortune-teller, but I can tell that the outlook is a bit bleak. Seeing how the world is so interwoven, and that disasters are portrayed completely falsely by those at the top, makes it somewhat difficult to stay positive about our food supply.

You can do something about this. You aren't stuck with this doomsday prognosis. You can take control of your destiny and start preparing for the future. This book has spent a considerable amount of time looking at different ways to get ready for a food shortage.

You can choose to can, dehydrate or freeze-dry your own food, or choose to just purchase the food each time you go to the grocery store. There are many companies, like ours at SurvivalCaveFood.com that offer premade foods perfect for saving time and money for a food shortage emergency.

It is up to you to show some concern for the future. Things are in a delicate balance and you can't rely on government officials, or other countries, to take care of you. Starting your food storage stockpile right now can keep you from starvation, help you to avoid panic, and will help your whole family stay happily well-fed until the situation gets sorted out.

Now is the time to prepare

While I can't tell you when this problem will come to head, I can tell you it'll probably happen when you least expect it. Preparing now is the thing to do so that you will have food to last you through tough times. It is much better to be prepared, way before you need the emergency food supply, rather than discovering you need the food tomorrow or you starve.

Get prepared for all disasters and emergencies today. This book is perfect for helping you to prepare for every possible food shortage circumstance while also explaining why this kind of storage is so important.

Visit us at survivalcavefood.com or feel free to contact our office at 800-719-7650 with any questions you may have.

Thanks and stay prepared....

J.R. Fisher

Appendix

Find out more information about the topics in this guidebook. Here are some great resources to help you get started!

Chapter 1:

http://www.silkroadspices.ca/history-of-spice-trade

Chapter 2

http://www.u-s-history.com/pages/h1601.html

http://www.wisegeek.com/how-is-the-world-connected-into-a-global-economy.htm

http://www.nytimes.com/interactive/2015/business/international/greece- debt-crisis-euro.html?_r=0

http://theeconomiccollapseblog.com/archives/the-financial-collapse-of-greece-the-canary-in-the-coal-mine-for-the-global-economy

Chapter 3

http://www.infowars.com/food-shortages-or-globalist-depopulation-agenda/

http://www.historyplace.com/worldhistory/famine/after.htm

http://www.bbc.co.uk/history/british/victorians/famine_01.shtml

http://www.statista.com/statistics/183657/average-size-of-a-family-in-the-us/

Chapter 4:

http://www.libertynewsonline.com/article_301_32849.php

http://economyincrisis.org/content/made-america-owned-china

http://www.smithfieldfoods.com/our-brands

http://money.cnn.com/interactive/economy/chinese-acquisitions-us- companies/

http://www.pilotonline.com/business/consumer/avoiding-chinese-owned- foods-it-s-not-that-simple/article_cb89a343-a7a2-5f94-adc2- d335acb677a0.html

http://www.theepochtimes.com/n3/231731-top-5-imported-foods-from-china-you-should-avoid/

http://www.nbcnews.com/health/health-news/pet-treat-mystery-more-dogs- dead-3-people-sick-fda-n107286

Chapter 5:

http://www.history.com/topics/russian-revolution

http://borgenproject.org/food-riot/

http://www.history.com/topics/french-revolution

Chapter 6:

http://www.weatherforkids.org/hurricanes.html

http://web.mit.edu/12.000/www/m2010/finalwebsite/katrina/government/government-response.html

Chapter 7:

http://www.u-s-history.com/pages/h3706.html

Chapter 8:

https://www.fbi.gov/about-us/investigate/terrorism/terrorism-definition

http://www.choicesmagazine.org/2007-1/grabbag/2007-1-12.htm

http://www.cfr.org/homeland-security/targets-terrorism-food-agriculture/p10197

http://www.voanews.com/content/us-iraq-likely-to-face-severe-food-shortages-because-of-conflict/1964519.html

http://www.drskillas.com/A-war-and-terrorism.htm

Chapter 9:

http://www.areyouprepared.com/7-Steps-to-Food-Storage-s/144.htm

http://www.areyouprepared.com/Food-Storage-Calculator-s/109.htm

Chapter 10:

http://www.areyouprepared.com/

Chapter 11:

http://www.secretsofsurvival.com/survival/top-10-high-calorie-foods.html
https://www.survivalcavefood.com/

http://everydaylife.globalpost.com/freezedry-things-40811.html

http://www.backdoorsurvival.com/food-storage-tips-for-the-space-challenged-prepper/

Chapter 12:

http://www.offthegridnews.com/off-grid-foods/how-to-stockpile-full-meals- for-emergency-situations/?fb_source=pubv1

http://iowasue.blogspot.com/2011/07/home-canned-meatballs.html

Chapter 13:

http://www.gardenguides.com/97478-tools-start-indoor-gardens.html

http://greatist.com/health/best-plants-to-grow-indoors

http://www.decoist.com/2012-05-24/indoor-gardening-ideas-to-beautify- your-space/

Chapter 14:

http://www.ehow.com/slideshow_12217504_foods-canning.html#slide=10

http://www.offthegridnews.com/off-grid-foods/the-best-vegetables-for-preserving/

http://www.simplebites.net/canning-101-the-basics/

Chapter 15:

https://www.survivalcavefood.com/

Made in USA - Kendallville, IN
1162504_9781542596800
09.10.2020 0855